Miso and Soy Sauce
for Flavor and Protein
Previously published as *Soybean Diet*

Herman and Cornellia Aihara

George Ohsawa Macrobiotic Foundation
Chico, California

Publisher's Notes: The 1974 edition of this book was written well before the introduction of genetically modified foods (GM foods) that are produced from genetically modified organisms (GMOs). Many people believe such foods are unsafe for human consumption. We recommend avoidance of all GM foods. References in this book to soybeans and all soy products are to those foods that contain no GMOs.

In recent years, researchers have expressed some concern about the trypsin inhibitor in soybeans. Trypsin is an enzyme in the pancreatic juice that helps in processing proteins. Fermenting soybeans with an inoculant removes this inhibitor. Miso, soy sauce, tofu, and natto are soy products that have the trypsin inhibitor removed and are highly recommended for healthy diets.

This book is made possible through a generous donation on behalf of Chandler J. Nelson.

Edited by Kathy Keller
Cover and text design by Carl Ferré

First Edition	1972
Second Edition	1974 Nov 1
Third Edition	2013 Jul 1

Published with the help of East West Center for Macrobiotics
    www.EastWestMacrobiotics.com

ISBN 978-0-918860-72-9

Contents

Preface

In the early 1960s when I was working at Chico-San Inc., which was at that time the sole manufacturer and distributor of macrobiotic foods in this country, I made a sales trip around the Bay Area every week carrying samples of miso, soy sauce, seaweeds, and other products. In every store I visited, I had to explain what miso or tamari (traditional soy sauce) was, because not one store owner had ever heard about them.

Now thousands of families in the United States eat miso soup daily, even for breakfast. Miso is used in the preparation of a variety of other dishes as well. Soy sauce has become a household word in macrobiotic and non-macrobiotic homes alike, and it is used daily in homes and restaurants throughout the country to season foods served at each meal.

Letters are received daily at the George Ohsawa Macrobiotic Foundation (G.O.M.F.) asking for more information about these products, especially about how they may be prepared at home. Included in this macroguide are recipes for miso, soy sauce, agé (deep fried tofu), and natto; each recipe has been adapted for home preparation. Recipes using each of these soybean products may be found in *Do of Cooking* published by G.O.M.F. More information about tofu, along with step-by-step illustrations for the home preparation of tofu, may be found in the same cookbook and later in this book on pages 112-113.

Acknowledgments

The following books have been used as reference and a source of information. I acknowledge my deepest appreciation for their work and cooperation giving us permission to use their work.

1. *Soybean* by Folke Dovring from Scientific American.

2. *The Yearbook of Agriculture* by U.S. Government, Dept. of Agriculture, 1959, February, 1974.

3. *Oriental Methods of Using Soybeans As Food* by Agricultural Research Service, U.S. Dept. of Agriculture.

4. *Protein vs. Protein* by Ida Honorof, published in the National Health Federation Bulletin, March, 1974.

5. "Minimum Daily Requirement of Amino Acids" taken from *Proteins* by Aaron M. Altschul, published by Basic Books, Inc., N.Y., 1965.

6. *Textbook of Biochemistry* by E.S. West, et al, published by MacMillan Co., N.Y., 1961, 1965, 1966.

7. *Amount of Essential Amino Acids* by the Japanese Scientific Research Council.

8. "Soybeans," *Encyclopedia Britannica*, published by Helen Hemingway Benton.

9. *Diet for a Small Planet* by Frances M. Lappe, published by Ballantine Books, N.Y.

10. *Macrobiotic Monthly* by G.O.M.F.

11. *Do of Cooking* by Cornellia Aihara, published by G.O.M.F.

12. *Health Food Business Review*, July, 1968.

Introduction

Since the first edition of *Miso and Tamari* was published two years ago, foods and the economic situation of the world as well as the United States have changed considerably. I have received letters asking how to obtain Miso Koji, or Koji seed (the substance needed to make Miso culture) which we don't have in this country. A few health food distributors are now importing Mugi Koji (fermented barley). This is a substitute for Miso Koji and makes it much easier to prepare Miso. Therefore, information on how to make Miso using Koji should be available. This is one of the reasons why I have revised *Miso and Tamari*.

I have added over 100 delicious recipes for soybean foods in this revised edition. They are recipes made by my wife Cornellia, who has been teaching macrobiotic cooking since 1960 in this country. She cooks without synthetics, chemical additives, and sugar. However, her cooking is not primitive and crude, but feminine, delicate, and tasty. Her cuisine is balanced. Her diet is a balanced diet. Her cooking and these recipes have been tasted by thousands of Americans throughout the country. The meals were found delightful by everyone.

The reason for adding recipes in this book is that soybeans will be more and more important for the future American diet. And yet most Americans do not know how to cook these delicious foods because until recently, America has been neither producing nor eating large quantities of soybeans. Now, however America has the highest soybean production rate in the world.

Americans have to reduce their meat consumption in order to import gasoline as Folke Dovring warned in *Scientific American* (February, 1974). This is true not only for gasoline; most Americans will not be able to buy as much animal food because the price will go up so much. In this event, soybean foods will be indispensable due to their high content of essential amino acids.

Americans are eating too much animal protein due mostly to advertisements by mass media that advocate the necessity of animal protein. The excess protein we consume turns to energy. This, when combined with other high energy foods such as sugar and sugary foods, makes Americans hypersensitive, nervous, and overactive, if not violent. In order to solve these problems, Americans must learn how to live consuming less animal foods. However, Americans who are brainwashed by modern nutrition theory are afraid to eat without meat or milk. In order to convince them of the adequacy of vegetable protein and essential amino acids they will be getting, I calculated the amount of protein and essential amino acids for each recipe according to Minimum Daily Requirement percentages.

In short, this book will show you how to make soybean foods and how to cook soybean foods. Furthermore, one who serves these dishes can know how much protein and what percentage of the M.D.R. of essential amino acids each person is getting.

Those who read this book should read other cookbooks written by Cornellia Aihara: *Do of Cooking* and *Calendar Cookbook* published by G.O.M.F. and the *Chico-San Cookbook* published by Chico-San.

I am most grateful to the people who helped me publish this book: Carl Campbell and Roy Collins for their lovely drawings, Jim Ledbetter and Carol Mead for their typing, Fred Pulver for his layout, Pat Chamburs for his proofreading, Joe Adamson for printing, collating, and binding. The recipes are a gift from my wife who cooks at Vega Institute every day early morning to night, giving tremendous joy and energy to everyone who comes there. Also I am grateful to Jean Karp of Idaho who advised me to read an article on soybeans in the *Scientific American* February 1974, which inspired me to write this revision.

CHAPTER 1

Theory

1. Steaks vs. Gasoline

"The American," Folke Dovring says in *Scientific American*, February 1974, "may have to choose between steaks and pleasure trips." How does eating steaks affect gasoline supply? Why does eating meat cause the shortage of gasoline? He explains thoroughly in the magazine. He says, "At present the U.S. is paying for its import (including meats as well as petroleum) by exporting soybeans, wheat, corn and other raw agricultural products. If the upward trend in meat consumption continues, however, to rise, petroleum imports can be expected to rise, too. In other words, the trend in meat consumption and energy consumption is on a collision course."

Although animal food consumption by Americans is decreasing, in 1971 Americans consumed 1.5 times more animal foods than grains, vegetables, and potatoes combined. The same year Americans consumed a total of 39,168 million pounds of animal foods (excepting fish). If Americans consumed half the amount of animal foods and substituted soybean products to get the same amount of protein, we would have eaten 21,000 million pounds of soybeans. However, land which produces 19,000 million pounds of animal food (which is half the amount of animal foods Americans consumed in 1971) will yield about 400,000 million pounds (200 million tons) of soybeans. This amount is almost 5 times as much as the total soybean production in the U.S. in 1971.

In other words, if Americans ate half the amount of animal foods they do now, America could export about 5 times the amount of soybeans as at present. In January 1973, this amounted to 3 billion dollars or more than 5 percent of all U.S. exports. Of course, this calculation is based on the assumption that all grazing lands can be converted to soybean fields. If this assumption were correct, the total increase of export will be 15 billion dollars, which is more than one third of the total U.S. export in 1973.

Chart I
Recommended Daily Dietary Allowance of Protein
Food and Nutrition Board, National Research Council (1958)

	Age (years)	Weight (pounds)	Protein (grams)
Men	25	154	70
	45	154	70
	65	154	70
Women	25	128	58
	45	128	58
	65	128	58
Pregnant (2nd half)			+20
Lactating (28 oz daily)			+40
Children	1-3	27	40
	4-6	40	50
	7-9	60	60
	10-12	79	70
Boys	13-15	108	85
	16-19	139	100
Girls	13-15	108	80
	16-19	120	75

Civilian Consumption of Major Foods per Person in Unit Lbs.
Economic Research Service, Dept. of Agriculture

Averages	1957-1959	1970	1971
Meats	156.6	186.3	191.8
Fish	10.5	11.8	11.2
Poultry products (assuming 8 eggs weigh 1 lb)	122.5	129.6	129.9
Dairy products	378.1	300.3	294.6
Total Animal	667.7	628.0	627.5
Grains	148.6	147.8	149.3
Vegetables	154.0	160.1	159.6
Potatoes	115.2	123.9	126.0
Total Non-Animal	417.8	431.8	434.9

2. Is Animal Protein Indispensable?

Reducing the amount of animal foods and substituting soybean foods will not only solve many problems of food supply, social, and world economy, but will also improve world health. If properly cooked, soybean foods make delicious meals. With this in mind, what are the factors that keep people from changing their diet?

The first reason is that many Americans are ignorant about the cooking methods and nutritional values of soybean foods. The other reason is that many believe blindly that animal foods are necessary and that vegetable foods cannot be substituted for them. It is the teaching of modern nutrition theory, and also commonly believed, that one must eat animal protein to maintain proper health.

People's belief that animal protein is indispensable is superstition. One can live without animal protein if provided with enough vegetable protein, except in very cold climatic places. Thousands of people are living with no animal protein. The following quotation from the U.S. government report on Chinese peasants proves this.

The high density of population in China dictates a vegetarian diet for most people, especially her peasants. I was informed by reliable authorities that customarily, the peasants of China eat meat only three times a year, on their three great holidays, the Dragon Festival, the Autumn Festival, and at their New Year's celebration. The farmers raise some chickens, ducks and pigs, and fish is common along the coast and waterways, but these products go largely to the few city people who can afford them.

According to Dr. William H. Adolph of Peking Union Medical College, the people of Northern China use a basic food combination consisting roughly of 40% corn, 40% millet and 20% soybeans. The Northern diet also contains much wheat, some rice and *Kaoliang* (sorghum wine).

A comparison of the Chinese and American diets according to Dr. Adolph is as follows:

Food	Chinese Diet (percent)	American Diet (percent)
Meat and Eggs	3.0	21
Fats and Oils	4.0	10
Milk	0.1	9
Sugar and Starch		10
Vegetables and Fruits	5.0	12
Cereals and legumes	88.0	38
Total	100%	100%

The division between animal protein and vegetable protein in the diet:

	Chinese	American
Animal protein	5%	55%
Vegetable protein	95%	45%

The diet in Northern China, even though it is mostly vegetarian, is quite well-balanced because of the wide variety of cereals and oil seeds it contains. Those who eat this in sufficient quantity show no outward evidence of undernourishment.

Dr. Adolph pointed out to me that the Chinese diet is much lower in calcium than the American diet, the difference being accounted for largely by the absence of cow's milk. The lower calcium intake of the Chinese is not generally apparent in their physical condition, and it has been suggested that their body systems have made a satisfactory adjustment to their available diet.

China gives a wonderful illustration of the effects on the human race of a vegetarian diet over a long period of time. In fact the state of nutritional equilibrium which has been attained in Eastern Asia on a vegetarian diet is unique and could no doubt serve as a source of valuable nutritional data.

Source: *Oriental Methods of Using Soybeans As Food* by the U.S. Department of Agriculture.

Folke Dovring supports this view in his writing on soybeans in the *Scientific American*, (February 1974). He says "Soy protein is nutritionally somewhat less complete than meat, but the few deficiencies can be made up easily from other vegetables including corn. A complete diet without animal products is therefore readily attainable."

Ida Honorof states in her article "Protein vs. Protein" in the *National Health Federation Bulletin* (March 1974) that, "Those who insist on the superiority and indispensability of meat base their arguments on both the large quantity and high quality of meat protein, and see plant protein as inferior on both counts, think of animal and vegetable protein as composing two separate categories. This is a great error."

Her thinking is very provocative and interesting: "Net Protein Utilization (NPU) values range from 40% to 94%. Animal protein occupies the highest position, but *meat is not at the top*. It places slightly above the middle with an average NPU of 67. Eggs are at the top (NPU of 94) and milk with an NPU of 82. The NPU of plant proteins generally ranges lower, between 40 and 70. However, protein quality (NPU) in soybeans and whole grain rice approach and even overlap the NPU values for meat."

"In conclusion," she says, "the general distribution of animal protein (high on the NPU scale) and plant protein (lower on the NPU scale) tells us that the proportion of essential amino acids found in most animal protein more nearly match human requirements than proportions found commonly in plants. This means that you need to eat proportionally less meat protein than plant protein to be assured of essential amino acid requirements."

3. Protein Requirements

Protein constitutes about 18.6 percent of total body weight and is ranked third by weight, following water and fat content. The protein intake is concerned not only with growth and maintenance after growth, but with several other life processes. Enzymes and certain hormones are protein and must be synthesized in the body from amino acids from ingested protein. The protein in blood, tissue fluids, intercellular and extracellular fluids affect the osmotic pressure, which in turn controls the amount of water. Scientists set daily requirements of protein but one must bear in mind that requirements may be altered by activity, temperature of environment, and conditions of organs.

From studies of the protein needs of dogs and from surveys of diets of moderately active men, Carl Voit suggested that the protein requirement for the average person is 118 grams, and 145 grams for the heavy laborer in 1881. An American nutritionist, Atwater, recommended 125 grams, which was the standard requirement of protein for several decades. David McCay in 1912 concluded in his study that the amount of protein contained in food contributes to a higher grade of muscle strength, durability, resistance to diseases, courage, and fighting spirit. In other words, a race that consumes more animal protein is stronger and more manly.

However, in 1901, Russell Chittenden of Yale University

claimed that the protein requirement should be reduced to ⅔. Horace Fletcher of *Fletcherism* observed a diet under the supervision of Dr. Chittenden consisting of 43 gm. of protein for several months and maintained 75 kg. of weight. He could even do heavy activity.

Chittenden did further experiments with 5 teachers, 13 soldiers, and 8 athletes, and analyzed their intake and excretions for 225 days. Chittenden concluded that one is able to maintain good health by consuming 36 grams of protein and 2000 calories of food energy daily. He maintained his weight at 125 pounds. Dr. Mendel maintained good health at 154 pounds with a daily consumption of 40 grams of protein. All the others also maintained good health on the low protein diet.

Chittenden concluded that:

1. Protein cannot be stored in our body tissues.

2. Our body will waste energy with excess protein intake.

3. Excess protein will create toxins by putrefaction (of animal protein), or fermentation (of vegetable protein).

4. Protein is not necessary as an energy source because carbo-hydrates and fats do the job efficiently.

6. It is necessary to take animal and vegetable protein in good proportion.

Today the scientists differ in their opinions on the amount of protein required for good health. According to the report of the World Health Organization, the requirements of protein for the average adult is 0.59 grams per kilogram of body weight. If one person weighs about 130 pounds, he must take 36 grams of protein per day.

The quantitative dietary protein requirement of man is still a matter of controversy. This is due largely to the difficulties involved in human nutritional experimentation, as said in *Biochemistry* by Edward Stanton West et al.

The scientists of the Food and Nutrition Board of the National Research Council have evaluated the results obtained by the many investigators who have studied hundreds of normal men and women and children (Chart I). On that basis, the Board has set up recommended daily dietary allowances designed for the maintenance of good nutrition of healthy persons in the United States. The Board has done this for all nutrients about which there is enough information.

Source: *Yearbook of Agriculture*, U.S. Government

The recommended amounts of protein include the amount indicated by the nitrogen balance studies plus an amount (usually about 50 percent) to cover individual variations in requirements of normal people and possible differences in the protein quality of foods selected by different people. (ibid.)

The earlier work on dietary protein was concerned primarily with the quantity in the diet. However, due to the improvement of knowledge recently, the quality of the protein is becoming rather important. This idea is the result of the discovery that protein is formed of various amino acids, that some amino acids are not synthesized in our body, and that protein value depends largely on the presence of specific amino acids.

Therefore, when considering the nutritional requirements of man, the requirement for specific amino acids (the so-called essential amino acids) should be considered, not just protein.

4. Essential Amino Acids—Law of All or Nothing

About 20 amino acids are common in our food. Eight of them are called essential because the body cannot make them itself from any materials. Our food must supply them completely formed and ready for use. They are tryptophan, threonine, phenylalanine, lysine, valine, isoleucine, methionine, and leucine.

Other amino acids can be manufactured by the body when necessary. They are glycine, tyrosine, cystine, cysteine, alanine, serine, glutamic acid, aspartic acid, arginine, histadine, proline, and thyroxine.

The *Yearbook of Agriculture 1959* states "Often the protein in grains, nuts, fruits, and vegetables are classed as partially complete or incomplete because the proportionate amount of one or more of the essential amino acids is low, or because the concentration of all the amino acids is too low to be helpful in meeting the body's needs."

The *Yearbook* considers that meat, fish, poultry, eggs, milk, cheese, and a few special legumes contain complete protein.

According to food analysis, those animal foods contain larger amounts of essential amino acids than vegetable, grain, or legume sources. However, the proportion of amino acids in vegetable sources is better. Some amino acids contained in animal foods are present in extremely high amounts. The excess of such amino acids are not used to build our body protein. Also, as the *Yearbook* points out, "Oversupply of one amino acid may reduce the utilization of another amino acid so that a deficiency will occur. Also, an excess of one amino acid may increase the requirement for another acid. The high leucine content of corn, for example, may increase the requirement for isoleucine."

Essential amino acids are like the building materials of a house—wood, cement, nails, metals, etc. Shortage of one material will stop the whole process of construction of the house. And the proportion of the amount of each needed material is important. If the construction requires 100 2" x 4", 100 of 1" x 4", 100 pounds of cement, and 1,000 pounds of nails, then 900 pounds of nails will stop the construction, and 100 pounds of cement will be wasted, if other materials cannot be obtained. Furthermore, those materials must be present more or less at the same time. This circumstance is more critical in the case of essential amino acids.

Dr. Paul Cannon of the University of Chicago experimented with rats, giving rats a ration of amino acids divided into two portions:

One contained half the essential amino acids. A few hours later he fed the other portion which contained the rest of the amino acids. The results proved that the animals needed all of the amino acids present at the same time.

Source: *Yearbook of Agriculture, 1959*

Dr. Cannon summarized his findings in this way: "The synthesizing mechanisms operate on an all-or-none principle and are perfectionistic to the extent that if they cannot build a complete protein, they will not build at all." (ibid.)

The *Yearbook of Agriculture 1959* claims that the same principle holds true for the human body, which was demonstrated in research at the University of Nebraska.

Another particular character of amino acids is that they do not stay single for long. Protein in food is broken down by the enzymes in the gastrointestinal tract into single amino acids, which are absorbed from the intestine and carried by the blood to the liver. As soon as they leave the liver, they are carried by the blood to different tissues. Here they are assembled into the special combinations that make the proteins that replace cell material that has worn out, or are added to tissue that is growing, or used to make some enzyme or hormone.

Any amino acids that are left over cannot be stored in the body for use at a later time. They are returned to the liver. The nitrogen leaves the body chiefly as urea through the urine, but the carbon, hydrogen, and oxygen fragments that are left can be used to provide energy. If the energy is not needed immediately, the fragments can be converted to fat and stored for use at a later time.

Then what proportion is best for the essential amino acid content of foods? To find the best proportion of essential amino acids in the foods of man, we have to find out what is the minimum daily requirement of essential amino acids.

5. Minimum Daily Requirement of Essential Amino Acids

According to the *Yearbook of Agriculture, 1959,*

Minimum requirements for the essential amino acids are determined by nitrogen-balance studies similar to those described for studies of protein needs. Instead of using foods as a source of the amino acids, however, the investigator has to feed the acids as purified chemicals. Only in that way can he single out one amino acid at a time from the others, and accurately measure and control the intake. Here, as with the protein studies, nitrogen is the index of the amount of an amino acid involved in the body's metabolism.

The experimental diet in the studies was no ordinary bill of fare. It could not include any foods that contained protein. Almost every kind of ordinary food, therefore, was ruled out. The menu was a variety of purified foods—purified cornstarch, sugar, and fat, plus vitamins and minerals. To this basic diet was added a solution of the amino acids in their chemically pure forms, and some extra nitrogen in a simple chemical for the body to use in making the non-essential amino acids.

Such a test diet cost about 25 dollars a person per day, but the cost did not keep the amino acids from being mildly distasteful. The diet was terribly monotonous. It was adequate nutritionally, but it was a poor substitute for meat and vegetables, milk, bread, and other foods the students would have liked. Sometimes the students were on the nitrogen-balance study for as long as 60 days while the intake of one of the amino acids was reduced gradually to find the least amount which would keep them in nitrogen equilibrium.

In the following chart (II), the Minimum Daily Requirements are shown. The requirements suggested by the Food and Agriculture Organization of the United Nations (1967) are shown in mg. per day by weight (note 2). When these values are converted for a man weighing 70 kg. (154 lbs), the value is a little lower than the suggested requirement presented by the National Research Council.

Recommendations by the National Research Council are the same as the requirement recommended by Rose, W.C. and his associates. Rose's experiments, however, do not show one requirement for each amino acid but, instead, show a large variation. Rose chose the highest value of the range as the minimum requirement. This is shown in note/column 11.

Although requirements by Rose and his associates took higher values according to experimental results that are shown in 11, the lower values (10) may be suitable for many. Another problem is

Chart II

Some average minimal daily requirements of amino acids for humans taken from table 9-1 of *Proteins: Their Chemistry and Politics*, by Aaron M. Altschul, copyright by Basic Books, Inc., New York, 1965.

Amino Acid	Infants			Adult Men			Adult Women		
	gm/Kg[1]	gm/Kg[2]	gm/Kg[3]	gm/Kg[2]	gm/Kg[4]	gm/Kg[1]	gm/Kg[10]	gm/Kg[11]	gm/Kg[1]
L-Histidine	.032		.034				.032		.034
L-Tryptophan	.022	.030	.022	.0029	.203	.250	.150	.250	.157
L-Threonine	.060	.060	.087	.0065	.455	.500	.300	.500	.305
L-Isoleucine	.090	.090	.126	.0104	.730	.700	.650	.700	.450
L-Leucine	.150		.150	.0099	.690	1.100	.500	1.100	.620
L-Lysine	.105	.090	.103	.0088	.615	.800	.400	.800	.500
L-Methionine	.085[5]	.085	.045[6]			.200[7]			
L-Methionine & L-Cystine				.0131	.925	1.100	.800	1.100	.550
L-Phenylalanine	.090	.090[8]	.090[8]	.0133	.935	.300[9]	.800	1.100	
L-Phenylalanine & L-Tyrosine						1.100			1.120
L-Valine	.093	.085	.104	.0088	.615	.800	.400	.800	.650

Chart II Notes

1. *Evaluation of Protein Nutrition*, Publication 711 (Washington, D.C., National Academy of Science—National Research Council 1959).

2. *Protein Requirements, Nutritional Studies, No. 16* (Rome, Italy; Food and Agriculture Organization of the United Nations, 1957).

3. L. E. Holt, Jr., P. Gyorgy, E. L. Pratt, S. E. Synderman and W. M. Wallace, *Protein and Amino Acid Requirements in Early Life* (New York, New York U.P., 1960). The requirements for histadine were later found to be less, closer to .023 gm/Kg.

4. Calculated from data in column 2 to the left for a man weighing 70 Kg (154 lbs)

5. No cystine was given. With cystine present at .050 gm/Kg, the methionine requirement was .065 gm/kg.

6. In the presence of cystine.

7. 810 gm/day of cystine were given.

8. Tyrosine was given.

9. 1.100 gm/day of tyrosine were given.

10. Rose, W. C. et al, *J. Biol. Chem. 217,1955* (for the lower range of requirements).

11. Rose, W. C. et al, *J. Biol. Chem. 217, 1955* (for the higher range of requirements).

---

methionine. Methionine and cystine are the only sulfur-containing amino acids. Cystine, which is not essential, is the helper for methionine. Since most foods (even animal protein) contain small amounts of methionine, calculating only methionine makes it difficult to establish the essential amino acid requirement and also makes food value charts inaccurate.

A similar relationship exists in the evaluation of phenylalanine. Tyrosine helps compensate for the shortage of methionine and phenylalanine; one must include the amount of these two non-essential amino acids in order to calculate the requirements of the essential amino acids. For this reason I used the requirement values given by

Chart III

Summary of Amino Acid Requirement of Man—All values were determined with diets containing the eight essential amino acids and sufficient extra Nitrogen to permit the synthesis of the non-essentials.

[Rose, W. C. et al., *J. Biol. Chem.*, 1955]

Amino Acid	Number of Quantitative Experiments	Range of Requirement Observed (gr. per day)	Value Proposed Tentatively As Minimum (gr. per day)	Value Which is Definitely a Safe Intake (gr. per day)	No. of Subjects Maintained in N Balance on Safe Intake or Less
1) L-Tryptophan	3[1]	0.15 - 0.25	0.25	0.50	42
2) L-Threonine	3[2]	0.30 - 0.50	0.50	1.00	29
3) L-Isoleucine	4	0.65 - 0.70	0.70	1.40	17
4) L-Leucine	5	0.50 - 1.10	1.10	2.20	18
5) L-Lysine	6	0.40 - 0.80	0.80	1.60	37[3]
6) L-Methionine	6	0.80 - 1.10[4]	1.10	2.20	23
7) L-Phenylalanine	6	0.80 - 1.10[5]	1.10	2.20	32
8) L-Valine	5	0.40 - 0.80	0.80	1.60	33

Chart 3 Notes

1. Fifteen other young men were maintained in Nitrogen balance on daily intakes of 0.20 g., though their exact minimal needs were not established. Of the 42 subjects maintained on the safe level of intake, 33 received 0.3 g. daily or less.
2. In addition to these three subjects, four young men received rations containing 0.60 g. of L-Threonine daily, and 16 others received doses of 0.80 g. daily. No attempt was made to determine the exact minimal requirement of these individuals, but all were in positive balance on the doses indicated.
3. Ten of these individuals received daily intakes of 0.80 g. or less.
4. These values were determined with Cystine-free diet. In three experiments, the presence of Cystine was found to exert a sparing effect of 80 to 89 percent upon the minimal Methionine needs of the subjects.
5. These values obtained with diets devoid of Tyrosine. In two experiments, the presence of Tyrosine in the food was shown to spare the Phenylalanine requirement to the extent of 70 to 75 percent.

(Taken from *Textbook of Biochemistry* by E. S. West et al., copyright by The MacMillan Co., N.Y., 1966, 1961, 1955.)

---

the National Academy of Science, which is shown in column 1 of Chart II. This recommendation includes the helping amino acids, cystine and tyrosine.

Without counting cystine, the minimum daily requirement for methionine is, according to most evaluations, 1100 mg. per day, which is one of the highest requirements of the essential amino acids. However, the amount of methionine contained in food is the lowest of the eight essential amino acids. Therefore, in order to satisfy the minimum daily requirement of essential amino acids, one must eat either a lot of food, or over one-half pound of meat. This may be the main reason nutritionists strongly recommend consuming animal foods and dairy products. However, in Asia, there are many who haven't been consuming much animal foods, as reported by the U.S. government (see page 12).

According to the study by the National Academy of Science, National Research Council, if cystine is present in the diet, a very small amount of methionine is required.

In the following chart (Chart IV), the smallest percentage of M.D.R. in a food is the limiting essential amino acid in that food.

When cooking, check these limiting amino acids and select other foods for which limiting amino acids have higher values, or different amino acid combinations. By proper combination, one can improve the percentage of the limiting amino acid, in other words, the value of the protein. For example, one cup of rice (uncooked) has enough protein to satisfy the Minimum Daily Requirement of essential amino acids (see Chart IV), except for Tryptophan, Lysine, and Methionine-Cystine. Methionine-Cystine especially represent only 42 percent of the requirement. Therefore, one cup of rice alone can satisfy only 42 percent of the requirement, even though the other amino acids are present in more than the necessary quantities.

Therefore, if the combination of foods eaten supply the additional 300 gms. of Methionine-Cystine, then one cup of rice can satisfy 70 percent of the requirement. By the same token, one egg will meet only 31 percent of the amino acid requirement because of methionine and cystine shortages. This will be increased by eating foods that contain methionine and cystine.

In Chart IV, I calculated the Minimum Daily Requirement (M.D.R.) percentage of various foods. The percentage obtained by comparison with the amount of each essential amino acid to each M.D.R. for adults (Chart II, column 1).

By this chart, one can find what percentage of M.D.R. is contained in certain quantities of foods. You will use this chart as a guide to make menus which will satisfy essential amino acid requirements.

The lowest number of M.D.R. percentage in each food (horizontal row), therefore, defines what percentage of the Minimum Daily Requirement we get from each food. I call this lowest value the limiting amino acid. In later chapters, I have calculated only the limiting amino acid and compared it with the M.D.R. so that one can estimate what percentage of the M.D.R. for essential amino acids one is getting.

Chart IV

Summary Amounts of Essential Amino Acids and Their Percentages with Minimum Daily Requirement in Various American Foods Based on Protein and Amino Acid Content of Foods in

The Yearbook of Agriculture 1959

Units in Grams

Food	Measure Weight/Unit	Protein	Tryp.	Thre.	Isol.	Leu.	Lys.	Meth.	Meth. Cys.	Pheny.	Pheny. Tyro.	Val.
MDR gm			0.25	0.50	0.70	1.10	0.80	.020	1.10	0.30	1.10	0.80
Milk, cow whole or nonfat fluid	244 gm/1 cup	8.50	0.12	0.39	0.54	0.84	0.66	0.21	0.29	0.41	0.84	0.59
MDR %			48	78	77	76	82	105	26	136	76	73
Milk, goat	244 gm/1 cup	8.1	0.10	0.53	0.21	0.68	0.76	0.16	0.16	0.30	0.30	0.34
MDR %			40	106	30	61	95	80	14	100	27	42
Milk, human	244 gm/1 cup	3.4	0.06	0.15	0.18	0.30	0.22	0.07	0.14	0.15	0.32	0.21
MDR %			24	30	25	27	27	35	12	50	29	26
Cheese, cheddar	1 oz	7.1	0.10	0.26	0.48	0.69	0.52	0.18	0.22	0.38	0.72	0.51
MDR %			40	52	68	62	65	90	20	126	65	63
Cheese, cottage	1 oz	4.8	0.05	0.23	0.28	0.52	0.40	0.13	0.17	0.26	0.52	0.28
MDR %			20	46	40	47	50	65	15	86	47	35
Cheese, cream	1 oz	2.6	0.02	0.12	0.15	0.20	0.20	0.06	0.08	0.16	0.28	0.15
MDR%			8	24	21	18	25	30	7	53	25	18
Eggs, whole, large	50 gm/1 egg	6.4	0.11	0.32	0.42	0.56	0.41	0.20	0.35	0.37	0.65	0.48
MDR %			44	64	60	50	51	100	31	123	59	60
Beef, medium, boneless	4 oz	20.6	0.24	0.91	1.08	1.69	1.80	0.51	0.77	0.85	1.55	1.15
MDR %			96	182	154	153	225	255	70	283	140	143

Food	Measure Weight/Unit	Protein	Tryp.	Thre.	Isol.	Leu.	Lys.	Meth.	Meth. Cys.	Pheny.	Pheny. Tyro.	Val.
MDR gm			0.25	0.50	0.70	1.10	0.80	.020	1.10	0.30	1.10	0.80
Chicken, fryer, fresh only	4 oz	23.4	0.28	0.99	1.23	1.69	2.05	0.61	0.92	0.92	1.74	1.15
MDR %			112	198	175	153	256	305	83	306	158	143
Fish	4 oz	20.6	0.21	0.89	1.05	1.56	1.81	0.60	0.88	0.77	1.33	1.10
MDR %			84	178	150	141	226	300	80	256	120	137
Lamb, leg, boneless	4 oz	20.4	0.26	0.93	1.06	1.58	1.65	0.49	0.76	0.83	1.54	1.01
MDR %			104	185	151	143	206	245	69	276	140	126
Liver, beef or pork	4 oz	22.3	0.34	1.06	1.17	2.06	1.67	0.53	0.81	1.13	1.97	1.41
MDR %			136	212	167	187	208	265	73	376	179	176
Pork, loin, boneless	4 oz	18.6	0.24	0.86	0.95	1.37	1.53	0.46	0.68	0.73	1.39	0.97
MDR %			96	172	135	124	191	230	61	243	126	121
Sausage, bologna	1 oz/1 slice	4.2	0.04	0.17	0.20	0.30	0.34	0.09	0.14	0.15	0.29	0.21
MDR %			16	34	28	27	42	45	12	50	26	26
Sausage, frankfurter	1/10 lb/1	6.4	0.05	0.26	0.31	0.46	0.52	0.14	0.22	0.23	0.44	0.32
MDR %			20	52	44	41	65	70	26	76	40	40
Sausage, pork links	2 oz	6.1	0.05	0.25	0.30	0.44	0.49	0.13	0.21	0.22	0.42	0.31
MDR %			20	50	42	40	61	65	19	73	38	38
Turkey, flesh only	4 oz	27.2	–	1.15	1.43	2.08	2.46	0.75	1.12	1.09	1.09	1.35
MDR %				230	204	189	307	375	101	363	99	168
Veal, round, boneless	4 oz	22.1	0.29	0.95	1.17	1.62	1.85	0.51	0.77	0.90	1.70	1.14
MDR %			110	190	167	147	231	255	70	300	154	142
Beans, common	1 oz	6.1	0.06	0.26	0.34	0.52	0.45	0.06	0.12	0.33	0.56	0.37
MDR %			24	52	56	47	56	30	11	110	51	46
Chickpeas	1 oz	5.9	0.05	0.21	0.34	0.44	0.41	0.08	0.16	0.29	0.49	0.29
MDR %			20	42	48	40	51	40	14	96	44	36

Food	Measure Weight/Unit	Protein	Tryp.	Thre.	Isol.	Leu.	Lys.	Meth.	Meth. Cys.	Pheny.	Pheny. Tyro.	Val.
MDR gm			0.25	0.50	0.70	1.10	0.80	.020	1.10	0.30	1.10	0.80
Lentils	1 oz	7.1	0.06	0.25	0.37	0.50	0.43	0.05	0.11	0.31	0.50	0.39
MDR %			24	50	52	45	53	25	10	103	45	48
Lima beans	1 oz	5.9	0.06	0.28	0.34	0.49	0.39	0.09	0.18	0.35	0.50	0.37
MDR %			24	56	48	44	48	45	16	116	45	46
Peas	1 oz	6.7	0.07	0.26	0.38	0.56	0.49	0.08	0.17	0.34	0.61	0.38
MDR %			28	52	54	50	40	15	113	55	47	
Soybeans	1 oz	9.9	0.15	0.43	0.58	0.84	0.68	0.15	0.34	0.54	0.88	0.57
MDR %			60	86	82	76	85	75	30	180	80	71
Soybean flour, low fat	101 gm/1 cup	45.1	0.68	1.98	2.66	3.81	3.12	0.66	1.54	2.44	3.01	2.59
MDR %			272	390	380	346	390	330	140	813	273	323
Soybean milk	4 oz	3.9	0.06	0.20	0.20	0.35	0.31	0.06	0.14	0.22	0.44	0.21
MDR %			24	40	28	31	38	30	12	73	40	26
Brazil nuts	1 oz	4.1	0.05	0.12	0.17	0.32	0.13	0.27	0.41	0.17	0.34	0.23
MDR %			20	24	24	29	16	135	37	56	30	28
Coconut, fresh	1 oz	1.0	0.01	0.04	0.05	0.08	0.04	0.02	0.04	0.05	0.08	0.06
MDR %			4	8	7	7	5	10	3	16	7	7
Peanuts	1 oz	7.6	0.10	0.23	0.36	0.53	0.31	0.08	0.21	0.44	0.75	0.43
MDR %			40	46	51	48	38	40	19	146	68	53
Peanut butter	16 gm/1 Tbsp	4.2	0.05	0.13	0.20	0.29	0.17	0.04	0.11	0.24	0.41	0.24
MDR %			20	26	28	26	21	20	10	80	37	30
Sesame meal	1 oz	9.5	0.16	0.35	0.47	0.82	0.29	0.31	0.55	0.71	1.18	0.43
MDR %			64	70	67	74	36	155	50	236	107	53
Sunflower meal	1 oz	11.2	0.17	0.44	0.62	0.85	0.42	0.22	0.45	0.59	0.90	0.66
MDR %			68	88	88	77	52	110	40	196	81	82

Food	Measure Weight/Unit	Protein	Tryp.	Thre.	Isol.	Leu.	Lys.	Meth.	Meth. Cys.	Pheny.	Pheny. Tyro.	Val.
MDR gm			0.25	0.50	0.70	1.10	0.80	.020	1.10	0.30	1.10	0.80
Barley	1 oz	3.6	0.05	0.12	0.15	0.25	0.12	0.05	0.12	0.19	0.32	0.18
MDR %			20	24	21	22	15	25	10	63	29	22
Bread	22 gm/1 slice	1.9	0.02	0.06	0.10	0.15	0.05	0.03	0.08	0.11	0.17	0.10
MDR %			8	12	14	13	6	15	7	36	15	12
Buckwheat flour	98 gm/1 cup	11.5	0.16	0.45	0.43	0.67	0.67	0.20	0.42	0.43	0.67	0.59
MDR %			64	90	61	60	83	100	38	143	60	73
Corn & soy grits	50 gm/1 cup	9.0	0.08	0.40	0.42	0.83	0.39	0.14	0.30	0.42	0.70	0.53
MDR %			32	80	60	75	48	70	27	140	63	66
Corn flakes	25 gm/1 cup	2.0	0.01	0.07	0.08	0.26	0.04	0.03	0.07	0.09	0.16	0.10
MDR %			4	14	11	23	5	15	6	30	14	12
Corn grits	160 gm/1 cup	13.9	0.08	0.56	0.64	1.80	0.40	0.26	0.44	0.63	1.48	0.71
MDR %			32	11	91	16	50	130	40	210	134	88
Corn meal, whole	118 gm/1 cup	10.9	0.07	0.43	0.50	1.41	0.31	0.20	0.34	0.49	1.15	0.55
MDR %			28	86	71	128	38	100	30	163	104	68
Oatmeal	80 gm/1 cup	11.4	0.15	0.38	0.59	0.85	0.42	0.17	0.42	0.61	1.03	0.68
MDR %			60	76	84	77	52	85	38	203	93	.85
Pearl millet	1 oz	3.2	0.07	0.13	0.18	0.49	0.11	0.08	0.12	0.14		0.19
MDR %			28	26	25	44	13	40	10	46		23
Rice, brown	196 gm/1 cup	14.8	0.17	0.58	0.70	1.27	0.58	0.27	0.47	0.74	1.40	1.06
MDR %			68	116	100	115	72	135	42	246	127	132
Rye flour, light	80 gm/1 cup	7.5	0.08	0.28	0.32	0.51	0.31	0.12	0.27	0.35	0.59	0.39
MDR %			37	56	45	45	38	60	24	115	53	48
Sorghum, grain	1 oz	3.1	0.08	0.11	0.17	0.50	0.08	0.05	0.10	0.16	0.25	0.18
MDR %			12	22	24	45	10	25	9	53	22	22

Food	Measure Weight/Unit	Protein	Tryp. 0.25	Thre. 0.50	Isol. 0.70	Leu. 1.10	Lys. 0.80	Meth. .020	Meth. Cys. 1.10	Pheny. 0.30	Pheny. Tyro. 1.10	Val. 0.80
Wheat flakes	35 gm/1 cup	3.8	0.04	0.12	0.17	0.31	0.13	0.04	0.11	0.17	0.28	0.20
MDR %			16	24	24	28	16	20	10	56	25	25
Wheat flour, whole	120 gm/1 cup	16.0	0.20	0.46	0.69	1.07	0.44	0.24	0.59	0.79	1.39	0.74
MDR %			80	92	98	97	55	120	53	253	126	92
Wheat flour, white	110 gm/1 cup	11.6	0.14	0.33	0.53	0.89	0.26	0.15	0.38	0.63	1.02	0.50
MDR %			56	66	75	80	32	75	34	210	92	62
Wheat germ	68 gm/1 cup	17.1	0.18	0.91	0.80	1.16	1.04	0.27	0.47	0.62	1.22	0.93
MDR%			72	182	114	105	130	135	42	206	110	116
Macaroni, elbow	123 gm/1 cup	15.7	0.18	0.61	0.79	1.04	0.51	0.24	0.54	0.82	1.34	0.90
MDR %			72	122	112	94	63	120	49	273	121	112
Noodles	73 gm/1 cup	9.2	0.10	0.39	0.45	0.61	0.30	0.15	0.33	0.45	0.68	0.54
MDR %			40	78	64	55	37	75	30	150	61	67
Shredded wheat	1 oz/1 biscuit	2.9	0.02	0.11	0.13	0.19	0.09	0.04	0.10	0.14	0.21	0.16
MDR %			8	22	18	17	11	20	9	46	19	20
Beans, lima	2 oz	4.3	0.05	0.19	0.26	0.34	0.27	0.05	0.10	0.22	0.37	0.27
MDR %			25	38	37	30	33	25	9	73	33	33
Cabbage	2 oz	0.8	0.01	0.02	0.02	0.03	0.04	0.01	0.03	0.02	0.04	0.02
MDR %			4	4	3	2	5	5	2	6	3	2
Carrots	2 oz	0.7	0.01	0.02	0.03	0.04	0.03	0.01	0.03	0.02	0.03	0.03
MDR %			4	4	4	3	3	5	2	6	2	4
Corn, sweet	2 oz	2.1	0.01	0.09	0.08	0.23	0.08	0.04	0.08	0.12	0.19	0.13
MDR %			4	18	11	20	10	20	7	40	17	16

MDR gm

Food	Measure Weight/Unit	Protein	Tryp.	Thre.	Isol.	Leu.	Lys.	Meth.	Meth. Cys.	Pheny.	Pheny. Tyro.	Val.
MDR gm			0.25	0.50	0.70	1.10	0.80	.020	1.10	0.30	1.10	0.80
Wheat flakes	35 gm/1 cup	3.8	0.04	0.12	0.17	0.31	0.13	0.04	0.11	0.17	0.28	0.20
MDR %			16	24	24	28	16	20	10	56	25	25
Okra	2 oz	1.0	0.01	0.04	0.04	0.06	0.04	0.01	0.02	0.04	0.08	0.05
MDR %			4	8	6	5	5	5	2	12	7	6
Peas, green	2 oz	3.8	0.03	0.14	0.17	0.24	0.18	0.03	0.07	0.15	0.24	0.16
MDR %			12	28	24	21	22	15	6	50	21	20
Potatoes	2 oz	1.1	0.01	0.04	0.05	0.06	0.06	0.01	0.02	0.05	0.07	0.06
MDR %			4	8	7	5	7	5	2	16	6	7
Spinach	2 oz	1.3	0.02	0.06	0.06	0.10	0.08	0.02	0.05	0.06	0.10	0.07
MDR %			8	12	8	9	10	10	4	20	9	9
Sweet potatoes	2 oz	1.0	0.02	0.05	0.05	0.06	0.05	0.02	0.04	0.06	0.11	0.08
MDR %			8	10	7	5	6	10	3	20	10	10
Turnip, greens	2 oz	1.6	0.03	0.07	0.06	0.12	0.07	0.03	0.06	0.08	0.14	0.08
MDR %			12	14	8	11	9	15	5	26	13	10
Gelatin	10 gm/1 T	8.6	00	0.19	0.14	0.29	0.42	0.08	0.09	0.20	0.24	0.24
MDR %			--	38	20	26	50	40	8	66	22	30
Yeast, compressed	1 oz	3.0	0.03	0.19	0.19	0.33	0.26	0.07	0.10	0.17	0.33	0.24
MDR %			12	38	27	30	43	35	9	56	30	30
Yeast, brewer's	8 gm/1 T	3.0	0.06	0.19	0.19	0.26	0.26	0.07	0.11	0.15	0.30	0.22
MDR %			24	38	27	23	43	35	10	50	27	27

Chart V

Amounts of Essential Amino Acids and Their Percentages with Minimum Daily Requirements in Various Japanese Foods Based on Analyses by the Japanese Scientific Research Council

Units in Grams

Food	Measure Weight/Unit	Protein	Tryp.	Thre.	Isol.	Leu.	Lys.	Meth.	Meth. Cys.	Pheny.	Pheny. Tyro.	Val.
MDR gm			0.25	0.50	0.70	1.10	0.80	.020	1.10	0.30	1.10	0.80
Soybeans, immature	100 gm	26.0	0.22	1.12	1.21	1.87	1.29	0.17	0.43	1.16	1.99	1.41
MDR %			88	224	172	170	161	85	39	386	180	176
Soybeans, mature	100 gm	34.3	0.55	1.62	1.80	2.70	2.58	0.43	0.91	1.98	3.36	1.86
MDR %			220	324	257	245	322	215	82	660	305	232
Tofu	100 gm	6.0	0.09	0.28	0.32	0.45	0.44	0.08	0.15	0.37	0.57	0.33
MDR %			36	56	45	40	55	40	13	123	51	41
Koya tofu (dehydrated)	100 gm	53.4	0.78	2.43	2.81	4.40	3.83	0.65	1.31	2.90	4.68	2.71
MDR %			312	486	401	400	478	325	119	966	425	338
Yuba (bean curd skin)	100 gm	52.3	0.78	2.84	3.02	4.30	3.02	0.79	1.21	3.02	5.02	3.30
MDR %			312	568	431	390	377	395	110	1006	457	412
Okara (residue from tofu)	100 gm	3.5	0.05	0.18	0.18	0.28	0.24	0.04	0.08	0.21	0.33	0.20
MDR %			20	36	25	25	30	20	7	70	30	25
Natto (fermented soybean)	100 gm	16.5	0.28	0.75	0.87	1.36	0.95	0.18	0.43	0.90	1.51	0.98
MDR %			118	150	124	123	118	90	39	300	137	122
Miso, rice	100 gm	12.6	0.18	0.66	0.86	1.28	0.53	0.19	0.27	0.53	1.02	0.75
MDR %			72	132	122	116	66	95	24	176	92	93
Miso, barley	100 gm	14.0	0.17	0.81	1.03	1.40	0.71	0.19	0.29	0.69	1.35	0.86
MDR %			68	162	147	127	88	95	26	230	122	107

Food	Measure Weight/Unit	Protein	Tryp.	Thre.	Isol.	Leu.	Lys.	Meth.	Meth. Cys.	Pheny.	Pheny. Tyro.	Val.
MDR gm			0.25	0.50	0.70	1.10	0.80	.020	1.10	0.30	1.10	0.80
Miso, soybean, hatcho	100 gm	16.8	0.26	0.82	0.94	1.34	1.09	0.20	0.36	1.00	1.68	0.97
MDR %			104	162	134	125	136	100	32	333	152	121
Soy sauce	100 gm	6.9	0.04	0.23	0.33	0.52	0.42	0.06	0.13	0.25	0.32	0.35
MDR %			16	46	47	47	52	30	11	83	29	43
Nori	100 gm	34.2	0.38	1.09	1.37	2.63	0.88	1.15	1.63	1.81	2.63	3.17
MDR %			152	218	195	239	110	575	148	603	239	396
Kombu	100 gm	7.3	0.13	0.21	0.27	0.43	0.21	0.13	0.25	0.33	0.60	0.57
MDR %			52	42	38	39	26	65	22	110	54	71
Hijiki	100 gm	5.6	0.04	0.18	0.38	0.40	0.16	0.18	0.25	0.32	0.49	0.56
MDR %			16	36	50	36	20	90	22	106	44	70
Wakame	100 gm	12.7	0.15	0.69	0.37	1.08	0.47	0.26	0.38	0.47	0.67	0.87
MDR %			60	138	52	98	58	130	34	156	60	108

Note: How To Use Chart IV & Chart V

Using these charts, you can calculate how much of protein, essential amino acids, and MDR (minimum daily requirement) you are getting in your meal. For example, if you cook a cup of brown rice and eat half of it with 3½ oz. (100 gm.) of natto, one sheet of nori, and a cup of miso soup, which may contain about ½ teaspoon of miso, then you will get the amount of protein and essential amino acids shown on the following Chart V'.

Because the lowest percentage of MDR of essential amino acids in your meal is 75 percent, you will be getting only 75 percent of MDR even though you are getting more than 100 percent MDR of other essential amino acids.

Although these charts are the result of intensive study and experiments, they show just averages but not the foods you eat. The quality of foods varies place to place, time to time, so don't rely on those data 100 percent. Your instinct or physical demand may be a more reliable source to follow. I am trying in this book to present a guide for your nutritious diet until you achieve fine instinct.

Another important consideration of your meal or cooking is the yin and yang grade of foods and the cooking method. However, I have no space to discuss yin-yang application to foods here, so I recommend you read other books, several of which are named in the bibliography.

Chart V'
Sample Meal Analysis
Units in Grams

Food	Measure Weight/Unit	Protein	Tryp.	Thre.	Isol.	Leu.	Lys.	Meth.	Meth. Cys.	Pheny.	Pheny. Tyro.	Val.
MDR gm			0.25	0.50	0.70	1.10	0.80	.020	1.10	0.30	1.10	0.80
Brown rice	1 cup	14.8	0.17	0.58	0.70	1.27	0.58	0.27	0.47	0.74	1.40	1.06
Brown rice	½ cup	7.4	0.08	0.29	0.35	0.63	0.29	0.13	0.23	0.37	0.70	0.53
Natto	100 gm (3½ oz)	16.5	0.28	0.75	0.87	1.36	0.95	0.18	0.43	0.90	1.51	0.98
Nori	1 sheet	3.4	0.04	0.11	0.14	0.26	0.09	0.12	0.16	0.18	0.26	0.32
Miso	½ tsp	0.33		0.02	0.03	0.03	0.02		0.01	0.02	0.03	0.02
Total eaten		27.63	0.40	1.17	1.39	2.28	1.35	0.43	0.83	1.47	2.50	1.85
MDR %		39%	160%	230%	190%	220%	160%	223%	75%	490%	270%	230%

CHAPTER 2

Miso

1. Introduction

Thousands of families in this country eat miso soup daily, even for breakfast. An article about miso was printed in the July 1968 issue of the *Health Food Business Review*. The article states:

> Miso soup, an integral part of eating for centuries in the Orient, is now an important mealtime essential for many. Miso soup is not just a lifted recipe from abroad, but a delightful, nutritious dish rich in vitamins and minerals. A food accepted because of its high protein value and its important function in helping digestion and assimilation. And a food that will be recommended more and more in the light of new evidence concerning the importance of carbohydrates and heart disease.

Miso soup served at breakfast with rice and pickles is an age-old custom of the Japanese. Its aroma is as appetizing for them as the aroma of coffee for Westerners. Miso and coffee both alkalize the blood and, therefore, wake up our nervous system. Both make men ready to work in the morning. However, miso soup is an energy-giver (yang) and coffee is an energy dispenser (yin). One should drink miso soup every morning instead of coffee, if one does not eat meat.

2. The Origin of Miso

The origin of miso is ancient. The people of China, as well as Japan, have been consuming miso for thousands of years. Dr. K. Misumi says in his book, *Miso Daigaku* (*Miso University*), that the Japanese miso originated at the beginning of the nation as the work of the Goddess Kuma-No-Kusubime-No-Mikoto. In other words, miso is the oldest staple food of Japan and has the same importance as rice in the Japanese diet. [*Rice and the Ten Day Rice Diet*, published by G.O.M.F.] In ancient Japan, miso was called "mushi" (a fermented food) and considered a medicinal food.

3. Kinds of Miso

There are many kinds of miso. They developed through local traditions because of the availability of ingredients and/or because of the taste desired. According to *Fermented Foods*, by S. Yamada and others, miso can be classified by its usage, ingredients, and composition. Regular miso is used for soup or in cooking other foods. Barley miso (Mugi Miso) is a product of soybeans, barley, salt, and water. Soybean Miso (Hacho Miso or Mame Miso) is made of soybeans, salt, and water. Lastly, Rice Miso (Kome Miso) is made of soybeans, rice, salt and water. Chart VI on page 37 differentiates "regular miso" and lists the varieties available and their characteristics. Name Miso is used as is, without cooking.

4. Ingredients

Soybeans are the main ingredient of miso. The soybean, also known as the soja bean or the soya bean in some countries, is an annual summer leguminous plant (*glycine soja* or *glycine mox*) native to eastern Asia and extensively cultivated in the U.S. Cultivated in China and Japan long before recorded history, it is, from the standpoint of uses and value, the most important legume crop grown in these countries. Many records of soybean culture are found in China as far back as 2207 B.C. Advice on soil preference, time of planting, varieties for different purposes, and numerous uses indicates that the soybean was among the earliest crops grown by man. The soybean crop was considered the most important cultivated legume and one of the five sacred grains (rice, soybeans, wheat, barley, and millet) essential to the existence of Chinese civilization. In a Chinese dictionary dating from about the beginning of the Christian era, the soybean is called *sou*, which very probably was the source of the name *soi, soy, soya,* and *soja*.

Chart VI

Regular Miso (Used with Cooking)

Kind of Miso	Variety Available	Characteristics
Kome miso (Rice miso)	Cherry miso	(1) High carbohydrate, high salt
	Saikyo miso (white)	(2) High carbohydrate, low salt
	Edo miso (red)	
	Sendai miso (red)	(3) Low carbohydrate, high salt
	Shinshu miso (white)	
Hatcho miso (Soybean miso)	Tamari miso	(3) Low carbohydrate, high salt
	Hatcho miso	
Mugi miso (Barley miso)	Mugi miso	(1) High carbohydrate, high salt
	Sweet mugi miso	(2) High carbohydrate, low salt
	Commercial mugi miso	(3) Low carbohydrate, high salt

Special Miso (Used on the Table without Cooking)

Kind of Miso	Variety Available	Characteristics
Name miso	Hishio miso	Miso with vegetables
	Meizanji miso	Miso with vegetables
	Tai miso	Miso with fish

Amount of Miso Production and its Raw Materials (Metric Tons)

Type of Miso	Annual Production	Amount Used			
		Soybeans	Rice	Barley	Salt
Factory made:					
Rice miso	379,000	134,000	72,000	--	58,000
Barley miso	146,000	52,000	--	30,000	22,000
Soybean miso	58,000	32,000	--	--	9,000
Total	583,000	218,000	72,000	30,000	89,000
Homemade:					
Miso, all types	391,000	143,000	43,000	38,000	70,000
Grand total	974,000	361,000	115,000	58,000	159,000

All Japan Miso Industrial Association,
Yearly report, Tokyo, 1956

Europeans first knew of the soybean through Engelbert Kaempfer, a German botanist who spent three years (1690 to 1693) in Japan. Kaempfer gave it the Japanese name *Daizu Mame* and described it as "an erect bean with the pod of a lupine and the seeds of a large pea." Although he discussed the many food products prepared from the soybean by the Japanese, little interest was taken in the soybean crop.

In 1875, a great impetus was given to soybean cultivation in Europe through the experiments of Friedrich Haberlandt of Austria who grew the seed of several varieties that were obtained at the Vienna Exposition in 1873. Seeds of the four varieties that matured were distributed widely in Austria-Hungary and other countries of Europe with promising results. In 1880, Vilmorin-Andrieus and Company introduced into France one of the yellow-seeded varieties that had been tested by Haberlandt. It proved to be well adapted to French conditions. Soybeans were grown as early as 1790 in the Royal Botanical Gardens, Kew, England, but the crop was not well adapted to the English climate, and there was no commercial production. Cultivation of the soybean in Italy dates from about 1840, but it still has not become an important crop in any part of Italy.

The first mention of the soybean in the U.S. was by James Mease, in 1804, who noted that it did well in the climate of Pennsylvania and recommended that it be cultivated. The Perry expedition to Japan, in 1854, brought back two varieties of "soya bean." For several years after that, the soybean was referred to as the "Japan pea." In 1882, a North Carolina Agricultural Experiment Station grew a yellow-seeded soybean, probably the Mammoth Yellow, which remained a leading variety in that area for many years. In 1889, W. P. Brooks of a Massachusetts agricultural experiment station brought from Japan a number of varieties. The next year, C.C. Georgeson secured three lots of soybeans from Japan and grew them at the Kansas agriculture experiment station. Since then, most of the agricultural experiment stations in the U.S. have conducted extensive tests with the soybean crop.

Chart VII
The Composition of Various Soybeans (%)

Location	Kind	Water	Protein	Fat	Carbo.	Fiber	Ash
Japan	Yellow	13.00	39.10	16.00	25.10	1.40	4.72
Japan	Black	13.30	36.40	15.90	23.90	4.30	5.13
Japan	Blue	11.40	35.70	17.50	26.00	4.20	4.48
Korea	Rynzan	12.43	39.15	21.28	29.49	5.04	5.04
Manchuria	Hakubi	09.64	40.52	17.13	14.33	5.44	4.52
U.S.A.		11.57	40.36	13.38	13.13	3.89	3.43

Chart VIII
Percent of Amino Acids in Glycine

Glycocol	1.00	Tryptophan	1.65
Leucine	8.45	Valine	0.68
Phenylalanine	3.83	Proline	3.78
Aspartic Acid	3.85	Tyrosine	1.85
Arginine	5.12	Glutamic Acid	19.46
Lysine	2.71	Histidine	1.39
		Cystine	1.12

In 1898, the U.S. Department of Agriculture began introducing large numbers of soybean varieties, mostly from Asian countries with a few from Europe and other parts of the world. Since then, the department has grown and evaluated about 10,000 varieties of foreign origin. Increase in acreage and production has been closely correlated with the introduction of these varieties and their improvement through breeding and selection.

The soybean will succeed on nearly all types of soils, but does best on fertile or sandy loams. Like other legumes, soybeans obtain part of their nitrogen requirement from the air through the action of certain nodule-forming bacteria living on the roots of the plant. Where soybeans have not been grown previously, it is advisable to innoculate the seed with soybean bacteria just before sowing. In the U.S., soybeans are usually planted during May or early June in rows thirty to forty inches apart. Early cultivations to kill small weeds or to break a soil crust are usually done with regular row equipment used for corn or cotton.

In Asian countries the soybean is grown primarily for the seed, which is used largely in the preparation of hundreds of fresh, fermented, and dried food products. These various food preparations not only give flavor to the Oriental diet but supply to a considerable extent the necessary protein in the diet. This has been especially true inland where seafood is not readily obtainable. Nutritionally, the protein of the soybean is similar to that of animal protein—even the amino acid analyses of soybean protein and casein are remarkably similar. Chart VII on page 39 lists the composition of various soybeans by percent.

The major protein in soybeans is glycine. Other proteins found are phaseolin, glutelin, and legumin.

The information in the table listing the percent of amino acids in glycine, on page 39, originally appeared in an article by T. B. Osborn in the *American Journal of Physiology* 19: 468,1907.

The soybean contains all of the essential amino acids. However, as Francis Moore Lappe pointed out in her book *Diet For a Small Planet*, the soybean contains less tryptophan and less of the sulfur-containing amino acids. Grains, conversely, contain high amounts of these amino acids but are low in isoleucine and lysine which is high in the soybean. Having exactly the opposite strengths and weaknesses, they, therefore, become a more complete protein when in combination. This is the reason that miso, made of soybean and grain, has so high a value as a source of essential amino acids.

Barley is the next most important ingredient of miso. Native to Asia and Ethiopia, it is one of the most ancient of cultivated plants or grasses. Its cultivation is mentioned in the Bible, and it was grown by the ancient Egyptians, the Greeks, the Romans, and the Chinese long before the Christian Era. Like other cereals, barley contains a large proportion of carbohydrates (67 percent) and of protein (12.8 percent). The annual production of barley in the U.S. totals about three hundred and fifty million bushels. Hordein and glutelin are the proteins found in barley. Barley contains 0.58 percent amino acids.

Composition of Hokkaido Barley

Water	Protein	Fat	Carbohydrate	Fiber	Ash
11.91	11.13	2.32	67.66	4.13	2.85

Rice, the next ingredient, consists of a considerably higher amount of carbohydrates and fewer minerals than barley. This fact, combined with the use of less salt, makes rice miso much sweeter than barley miso (mugi miso). Therefore, rice miso requires less fermentation time.

Commercialism, plus the Japanese craving for the sweet taste, have made rice miso so popular in Japan that within about the last half century most of the miso sold in markets has been rice miso. (This rice miso is mostly made of white rice.) Since rice miso contains more glucose and less minerals than barley miso, an anemic person or one who has trouble with intestines or lungs would do better, in my opinion, to eat barley miso rather than rice miso. We experimented for three weeks in my house with the use of rice miso bought from a Japanese food store in San Francisco. After three weeks, my wife started having chest pains and I began to have shoulder pains. After switching back to barley miso, both pains disappeared. However, rice miso made from brown rice would give a more positive result. Many Americans who have previously eaten much meat or who continue to crave much sugar will find that eating rice miso helps to balance meat and animal salts, which are yang and remain stored in the body for some time. In this way they substitute rice glucose for sugar.

After several years of a macrobiotic or vegetarian diet, one should discontinue the use of rice miso. However, occasional use of it will not be harmful if the rice miso is made of genuine whole rice, whole soybeans, and unrefined salt.

Composition of Rice
(From *Fermented Foods* by S. Yamada)

	Water	Crude Protein	Crude Fat	Carbo.	Crude Fiber	Mineral
Brown Rice (Japanese)	14.48	7.53	2.52	72.58	1.38	1.29
White Rice (Japanese)	13.86	6.33	1.00	77.70	0.25	0.48
Brown Rice (Chico-San Organic)	13.00	6.60	2.40		0.90	1.30

Salt from sun-evaporated ocean water is the best salt to use, but this may contain dirt. Therefore, cleaned crude salt would be the best to use in making miso. According to *Fermented Foods*, nonrefined salt has a better taste in miso. Rock salt or table salt contain fewer important minerals and will make miso too salty. Below is a table showing the composition of salt. I do not have available an analysis of the unrefined salt sold in this country, but I imagine that it would be close to the first one on the list that follows below.

Composition of Salt
(From *Fermented Foods* by S. Yamada)

	Water	NaCl	$CaSo_4$	$MgSo_4$	$MgCl_2$	KCl	u.p.*
Japanese							
boiled	8.762	85.477	1.365	1.669	1.572	0.572	0.104
vacuum	2.470	95.044	0.660	0.370	0.453	0.200	0.002
Formosan							
regular	4.634	92.900	0.947	0.418	0.483	0.142	0.172
fine	4.030	93,580	0.913	0.155	1.058	0.193	0.144
German							
rock	0.070	97.870	—	0.250	—	1.700	0.010

* u.p. = undissolved parts

Water used in making miso, according to S. Yamada, may either be hard or soft. However, one should avoid water contaminated with chemicals.

5. How To Make Miso
Translated here is the method of Dr. K. Misumi, an authority on miso making, from his book, *Miso University*.

(a) Barley Miso
Wash barley, then soak in double the amount of water for several hours. Then steam in a steamer. After it becomes soft, spread in flat wooden containers, which must be clean of any other bacteria. After it cools to body temperature, mix with miso bacteria (Miso Koji Seed), which is produced by Jozo K.K. and other companies, and is called by the brand name Marufuku Moyashi or No. M1.

Ingredients:
3.3 lbs barley
⅓ oz miso koji seed (bacteria *aspergillus aryzae*)
3.3 lbs soybeans
1 lb salt

Good miso bacteria is the most important factor in successful miso making. Macrobiotic food stores will carry them in the near future.

When you have no fermenting room, you can cover the barley and koji mixture with blankets. The fermentation continues for about forty-four hours and then the blankets can be taken off. Do not uncover sooner than the proper time of forty-four hours has elapsed.

While fermenting barley, soak soybeans in water for five to six hours. Then cook thoroughly for sixteen hours. After the soybeans soften, remove from the fire and let cool naturally. Next, grind the soybeans in a suribachi (mortar) with a wooden pestle after saving the cooking liquid. (A meat grinder may also be used for this process.)

Mix ground soybeans with the cooked juice and add salt. The amount of salt changes the quality of the miso and the taste. Less salt makes faster fermentation, but will create a less yang miso.

Guide to Illustration for Making Mugi Miso

Illustration Number:
- (1)   Soaking barley.
- (2)   Steaming barley.
- (3)   Adding Koji (enzyme) to barley.
- (4)   Natural fermentation in warm, moist room.
- (5)   Soaking and cooking soybeans.
- (6)   Mashing soybeans.
- (7)   Measuring and putting the cooked barley and mashed soybeans together. Measuring and adding salt to this.
- (8)   Mixing and stirring together.
- (9)   Fermentation over a period of time.

Finally, mix soybeans with barley koji that was fermented by bacteria in wood kegs. This miso can be eaten after approximately eight months. If three pounds of salt is used, the taste of the miso will be good after three years and can keep a long time. Of course, more salt will make a more yang miso.

(b) Rice Miso (Kome Miso)

Ingredients:
3.3 lbs rice
⅓ oz miso koji bacteria
3.3 lbs soybeans
1 lb salt

The process is the same as barley miso except that rice is used instead of barley.

(c) Soybean Miso (Hatcho Miso)

Ingredients:
3.3 lbs soybeans
⅓ oz miso koji bacteria
1 lb salt

Ferment cooked soybeans with miso koji bacteria as in the process for making barley miso or rice miso.

Soybean miso lacks the protein and carbohydrates of grains and it is not as delicious as barley miso. Because it contains less carbohydrates, it requires more time to make. This is the reason that soybean miso is more expensive than others, even though the quality is not better, as Dr. K. Misumi notes in his book, *Miso Daigaku.*

(d) Other Types of Miso

Various grains and beans can be used for miso. Black beans, aduki beans (red beans), lima beans, chick peas, etc. can be substituted for soybeans. However, the essential amino acid balance in such miso will not be as complete as in soybean miso.

Almost any kind of carbohydrate can be used in place of barley.

Analytical Comparison of Three Kinds of Miso

	Barley Miso	Rice Miso	Soybean Miso
Water	50.558	48.215	41.168
Protein	11.277	12.355	23.489
Crude salt	3.751	2.811	10.489
Dextrose	11.816	20.385	3.213
Carbohydrate	4.016	3.912	1.597
Salt	11.031	7.400	10.516
Ash	3.916	1.469	2.870
Crude fiber	1.956	2.069	3.980
Amino-Nitrogen	0.329	0.273	0.835
Total acid	1.350	1.094	2.475

A few of these foods are wheat, rice bran, millet, rice, rye, corn, oats, buckwheat, sweet potato, potato, albi, pumpkin, and squash. However, from the macrobiotic point of view, many of these will be too yin to use in miso except for the grains. Always be aware that there is a big area in cooking to investigate and in which to use your imagination.

(e) Miso Pickles

When making miso, you can make pickles, too. At the bottom of the keg, spread a layer of miso mixture. Then lay one layer of cucumber, eggplant, daikon, or carrot that has been pressed with salt. Place more miso mixture over the vegetables. These will become delicious, appetizing miso pickles in about 6 months to one year.

Note: prior to pickling, press vegetables in a container until excess water comes out of them, then drain.

6. Value of Miso

An article on miso appearing in the *Health Food Review*, July 1968, says that one cup of miso soup contains about 1 percent grams of fat and four grams of protein essential to normal activity and health. It is also recommended for the prevention of mineral deficiencies. Minerals neutralize acidity in the blood caused by oxidation. To prevent the body's mineral supply from being taken out of the bones and organs, daily replenishment of mineral requirements is necessary. Milk is taken by the young to fill this need in the very early years but later, toward adulthood, minerals are taken in the form of vegetables. By analysis, a pint (two cups) of milk contains about 300 mg. of minerals whereas a cup of miso soup with wakame (a sea vegetable) contains roughly 120 mg. of minerals.

The article went on to say that miso also contains many bacteria such as lactic bacteria. Bacteria in the small intestine digest and assimilate our food. If these bacteria are not present, even good food will not be utilized by the body. Miso soup provides, in this respect, bacteria that digest food. Furthermore, miso soup neutralizes poisons produced by excess animal food or supplements a diet where some animal food is required. In addition, other important health-giving nutrients present in abundance in miso are calcium, phosphorus, iron, potassium, magnesium; sulphur and copper are found in lesser amounts.

Although the above information points up the constituents of miso, it does not generate the excitement of considering miso in light of recent findings concerning the prevention of coronary heart disease (see page 50).

(a) Protein

As a source of protein, miso is excellent. Soybeans, which are the basic ingredient of miso, are called "vegetable meat." Soybeans contain 36 percent protein, 17 percent fats. Soybeans are very hard to digest even when they are cooked, roasted, or boiled. In miso, natto, and tofu (see later chapter), they are biologically transformed and the protein and fat can be digested easily. One cup of miso soup contains about four grams of protein. According to modern nutritional theory, vegetable protein is inferior to animal protein due to the fact that vegetable protein is not completely balanced in its amino acid content. In fact, protein from soybeans lacks certain amino acids that are essential. However, this deficiency can be corrected in miso by adding barley or rice.

In *Diet for a Small Planet*, Frances M. Lappe states that the "amino acid deficiency of soybeans appears in sulfur-containing amino acids. However, the amino acid deficiency of barley appears in isoleucine and lysine. It is now clear why legume protein, on the one hand, and the protein in grains, on the other hand, complement each other. Having exactly the opposite strengths and weaknesses, in combination they become more complete protein." Miso is one such combined food that increases usable protein by combining two sources of protein. This is the reason miso is a wonderful source of protein.

Miso is an excellent source of protein not only from the standpoint of protein usage but also its quality. Animal protein is not good. "Physiologically speaking," Dr. S. Akizuki says, "animal protein overworks the kidneys. Putrefaction of animal foods in the intestine produces poison and damages the heart, arteries, and nervous system. Animal protein also produces allergies as well as causing acidosis. Miso soup never produces these effects. Moreover, miso soup removes the putrefaction caused by animal protein."

(b) Fat

According to Dr. Akizuki, miso contains a sufficient amount of fat. He says that "Fat should be taken regularly, and it should not be taken in too large a quantity at one time. Excess fat is rather poisonous, if not a waste. The Japanese diet lacks fat compared with the Occidental diet. Therefore, miso soup with agé (fried tofu) is very important to them. Fish contains much fat. However, fat found in fish easily oxidizes, especially in summer. The same is true of butter and cheese. Foods such as these are not recommended in Japan between April and October, but miso is recommended all year long."

(c) Minerals

"During adolescence, the body excretes excess minerals. If the intake of minerals is less than the requirements of the body, the metabolism will consume the minerals from the organs, especially from the bones. The activity of the body is oxidation. In other words, when we exercise through thinking or walking or by other forms, such activities produce acid in our body. Our blood and body fluids must be alkaline so the acid from activity can be neutralized. Minerals produce this alkaline condition and are elements important for metabolism."

One pint of cow's milk contains about 300 mg. of minerals. This is more than is needed for humans. Such excess minerals may be deposited in joints of bones causing illness. One cup of miso soup with wakame, on the other hand, contains about 120 mg. of minerals. If you give miso soup every morning to your child, you can help prevent weak bones.

(d) Poison Prevention

Miso can prevent poisoning from smoking and alcohol drinking. Oxydized alcohol produces aldehyde which causes headaches or dizziness in cases of excess usage:

$$RCH_2OH + O \rightarrow RCHO + H_2O$$
$$\text{Alcohol} \qquad \text{Aldehyde}$$

Miso decomposes this aldehyde and eliminates it from the blood stream.

Nicotine causes the slowing-down of the contraction and expansion of the blood vessel movement, which results in poor blood circulation and can result in paralysis of the autonomic nervous system when absorbed in large amounts, such in the case of the heavy smoker. Miso will eliminate nicotine from the blood stream. Miso combines with nicotine and forms a compound that is easily eliminated from the body.

(e) Heart Disease

Miso contains linoleic acid and lecithin, which dissolve cholesterol in the blood and soften the blood vessels. Thus, miso will be a great help in preventing arteriosclerosis or high blood pressure.

(f) Miso for Beauty

Skin cells are replaced by underlying cells every day. Therefore, if underlying cells are not healthy, skin will not be healthy or beautiful. Underlying cells of skin are nourished by intercellular fluid and blood. Therefore, keeping cell fluid and blood healthy and alkaline is one of the secrets of having beautiful skin. Healthy cell fluid and blood are produced by good food. Miso is such a food because it contains blood-cleaning minerals and bacteria.

(g) Stamina

Miso contains a large amount of glucose, which gives us energy. However, miso differs from refined sugar because of its alkaline-forming characteristic. Glucose gives energy and alkalizes the blood. Therefore, miso is a wonderful source of energy and stamina.

(h) Miso for Radiation and Other Diseases

Miso contains, according to Dr. K. Morishita, zybicolin, which combines with radioactive substances and can be eliminated through the feces. Thus, miso is a useful food that can prevent radiation diseases.

Miso is also a good food for allergies, according to Dr. Morishita. He says that allergic diseases are caused by weak intestines that cannot transmute vegetable or animal protein to our own protein. In order to cure an allergic constitution we have to strengthen the function of the intestine so that it can transmute other types of protein to our own protein. Miso can do this due to the presence of many beneficial bacteria produced during fermentation, which aids in the breakdown of complex protein molecules.

In Japan, many investigations prove that miso soup is one of the main foods that contributes to longevity.

(i) Miso Soup

George Ohsawa said one bowl of miso soup for breakfast gives you enough energy for the entire day. After you have finished supper, do not eat anything else, so that when you go to sleep all of your food is digested. When you wake up, although you may be hungry, do some work first, then eat. This is orderly. Do this every day and it will make you beautiful and healthy. On an empty stomach, miso soup is very welcome. It makes you yang and gives you energy to do some work. All of the body cells are hungry; they take this yang food and change it to energy. If your stomach is very hungry and you eat sweet food, all of the cells become expanded, tired, and weak. You have no energy. You tire quickly and cannot be active all day. Try to use yin vegetables in miso soup, this makes the vegetables more yang. Do not use extreme yin vegetables such as eggplant because miso soup is watery, which is yin. Do not try to yangize quickly by taking a lot of miso soup. This makes you thirsty, and it is not a good idea to take so much liquid. For small children, add a little miso first, then take out the child's portion. Then add more miso for adults. If you do not need miso soup in the morning, you are drinking too much liquid. When miso soup is really welcomed by your body in the morning, then your condition is good.

When you can see the shape of the grain or soybeans in the miso, this is good. If the miso is too smooth, the bacteria have been somewhat destroyed by grinding. This is not good. Grind the miso yourself in a suribachi before adding it to hot soup. Always mix the miso with a little water or soup stock first to make the miso creamy. Never add it directly to the soup from the container. Most vegetables can be used for the miso soup, but they must be well cooked; for example, raw daikon can be irritating for someone with a sore throat. Be careful not to overcook. Two or three kinds of vegetables combined together make the best miso soup; also consider textures when you combine. If you are too busy in the morning, cook your soup the night before. Bring to a boil, turn down to a medium flame, and let the vegetables continue to boil gently. Cook until done (about 20 minutes). Either a higher or lower flame will cook the vegetables, but each will produce a different taste. Wakame is good for making a healthy body and many vegetables combine well with it. Also, try other kinds of seaweed in your cooking, not just in miso soup.

In preparing your daily vegetables, combine different varieties by color and smell; do not always use kombu or soup stock. Pumpkin cooked for a long time on a medium flame becomes very tender and sweet. It can be cooked on a higher flame for a shorter time, but the taste is not sweet. Vary the shape of the vegetables, cut them large or small. Make your cooking artistic and harmonious. For example, use left-over noodles, bread, or dumplings in miso soup. Left-over tempura batter can be mixed with flour to make soup dumplings.

Have more variety in your cooking. Prepare miso soup for any meal. After grinding the miso, add it to your boiling soup. After one bubble appears, shut off the flame and serve. If miso is boiled, the flavor goes away. If everyone is not present for dinner, save some soup without the miso, and add it when they arrive. It is best to serve when everyone is present. This brings more harmony and order into your life. You can serve miso soup with fish for supper, but for breakfast it is not so good. Vegetarian miso soup, which has a lighter feeling, is better in the morning. To serve miso soup, a Japanese porcelain bowl is the best. Everyone is delighted by such a beautiful bowl so they take special care of their soup. This miso soup gives your home vitality.

Some miso soup combinations:

onion and turnip
daikon and taro
spinach and scallion
cabbage and daikon
wakame and turnip
wakame and green vegetables
scallion and sweet potato
onion and cabbage
Chinese cabbage and carrot
dried daikon
dried daikon and spinach
Chinese cabbage and daikon
fu and scallion

burdock and scallion
squash and scallion
daikon and scallion
daikon and carrot
Chinese cabbage and turnip
carrot and turnip
albi and carrot
swiss chard and daikon
wakame and Chinese carrot
burdock and daikon
daikon and agé (fried tofu)
taro and scallion

Try some of these and other combinations for miso soup. For an adult, one heaping teaspoon of miso is the normal daily quantity; for children and old people, ½ teaspoon or one level teaspoon is adequate.

7. Miso in the Treatment of Tuberculosis and Atomic Radiation Exposure

A Japanese medical doctor, Dr. S. Akizuki of St. Francis Hospital, Nagasaki, Japan, not only cured his life-long illness but also prevented fatal illness from radiation when the atomic bomb exploded near the hospital in 1945. His article on the subjects was published in *The Macrobiotic Monthly, No. 5*, and is reprinted here. He wrote:

One day as I lay in bed ill with tuberculosis I decided to change my constitution. I knew I could cure my sickness, but I was not sure how to change my constitution. How was I to change my constitution? The answer was to change my diet. Although my parents did not farm, they lived in the countryside when they were about twenty years old. To the best of my knowledge they had never experienced any serious illness. If they caught a cold they cured it simply by taking a diaphoretic herb (an herb which makes you sweat). To stop diarrhea they took salt-plum tea. If I were to compare myself to them, I have had many very serious illnesses—whooping cough, diptheria, pneumonia, and tuberculosis of the lung. Even though my mother cooked miso soup for breakfast, my brothers, sister and I would eat fish or fish cakes instead. Fish was abundant in the seaside city of Nagasaki and vegetables were scarce, so my family stopped taking miso soup for breakfast. My mother gradually stopped making miso soup altogether.

My parents did not have an understanding of the importance of miso soup in the Japanese diet. Nutritional authorities recommended eggs, milk, or meat rather than miso soup. It was from the new diet that I became sick. I did not have much faith in miso soup in the beginning, but I was completely disappointed by Occidental medicine because no remedy had ever cured my sickness entirely. Then I decided to change my diet to brown rice, vegetables, and miso soup. It was war time and only a few Japanese medical doctors were available then. I was forced to leave my bed and carry on my duties as a physician. I was drafted even though I had tuberculosis. Then when the bombs exploded I was exposed to radiation sickness. However, I continued to work hard. My ability to overcome the hardship I had to endure I attribute to the eating of miso soup....

On August 9, 1945, the atomic bomb was dropped on Nagasaki. Lethal atomic radiation spread over the razed city. For
many it was an agonizing death. For a few it was a miracle. Not
one co-worker in the hospital suffered or died from radiation.
The hospital was located only one mile from the center of the
blast. My assistant and I helped many victims who suffered the
effects of the bomb. In the hospital there was a large stock of
miso and tamari (traditional soy sauce). We also kept plenty
of brown rice and wakame (seaweed used for soup stock or in
miso soup). I had fed my co-workers brown rice and miso soup
for some time before the bombing. None of them suffered from
atomic radiation. I believe this is because they had been eating
miso soup. How could miso soup prevent sickness from radiation? Someday science will answer that question conclusively
if people are allowed to provide data for experiments. I, myself,
would like to do such an experiment.

To improve my constitution I decided to live in the countryside. I overworked and came down with tuberculosis again.
I returned to Nagasaki to assume my medical duties as admin-
istrator of St. Francis Hospital. I included miso soup as a treatment for tuberculosis. I tried brown rice alone. Then vegetarianism, later adding dairy products, but this did not last long. I
continued to take miso soup. At that time Occidental medicine
had introduced many drugs for tuberculosis, such as strepto-
mycin and PAS (para-amino salicylic acid). These drugs were
introduced and proven to remedy many cases of tuberculosis.
Many improved surgical methods were also introduced. I applied these new drugs and new techniques of Occidental medicine to my patients. And I do not deny their effectiveness. Even
while applying these new medicines, I never forgot that *if a
man does not change his constitution, his sickness will never
be cured completely.* Whether the sickness is easily cured or
not is dependent upon the patient's constitution. Some improve
quickly, others find it difficult to improve, even while taking
the same drugs. In these cases the effectiveness of drugs depends mainly on the person's constitution.

I think that miso soup is the most important part of one's diet. Modern medicine recommends milk, eggs, tomato juice, etc. Miso soup, on the other hand, awaits evaluation. Few have considered studying the importance of authentic Japanese food. Whenever I see a patient, I ask whether he eats miso soup or not. It is very interesting. Most people answer that they do sometimes. Mothers complaining about their children's illness when asked whether or not they give their family miso soup always say no. They are more interested in giving them eggs and other Occidental food. This response comes especially from intelligent people. On the other hand, the family that is rarely sick always takes miso soup every day, with no exception. However, miso soup is not a drug such as a cortical hormone or an antibiotic. It does not cure sickness right away. If you are taking miso soup daily your constitution improves and you acquire resistance to sickness.

Occidental medicine has three categories: high, middle, and low. Low medicine is symptomatic treatment that removes symptoms through the use of drugs and such, but leaves side effects. Middle medicine is that which uses drugs but never has side effects even when continued for a long time. It removes symptoms but not their cause. High medicine is preventive medicine. Most modern medicine is low medicine. If not, then it fits into the medicine of the middle. Today people are never satisfied when a drug is not quickly effective. They appreciate morphine, thalidomide, and cortical hormones (adrenalin is a cortical hormone). I contend that miso belongs to the highest medicine. In my family we began to eat miso soup every morning. We continued to eat it for more than ten years. With this diet, I cured tuberculosis and chronic asthma effortlessly. However, I do not condemn milk, eggs, etc. Even I used antibiotics for my tuberculosis; but I do think that miso soup will restore the body more effectively than drugs.

People call miso a condiment; but miso is an agent which brings out the value from all foods. And it more easily allows the body to assimilate its food. The diet for a child is difficult.

Their tendency toward food is to go to extremes. If the diet is too strict, they become nervous. Therefore, in my family, I suggested that every morning they eat miso soup made with wakame (seaweed), agé (fried soybean curd), and vegetables. The rest of the diet I left up to their choice. The result was favorable. I recommended to parents at PTA meetings that they give their children miso soup every morning." (*Translated from Japanese by Herman Aihara.*)

8. How to Make Miso Using Mugi Koji (Fermented Barley)
Yields 100 pounds.

> 30 lbs (about 83 cups) soybeans
> 20 lbs (about 40 heaping cups) barley
> 15 lbs (about 25 cups) salt
> 7 cups mugi koji
> 8 koji boxes (18 in. x 24 in. x 3 in.)
> 20 gallon crock

Wash the barley until the water is clear, strain. Cover the barley with water; it should be covered 2 inches over the top of the barley. Soak for 7 hours. With your fingernail, test the softness of the barley; if it breaks easily it is done, if not, soak longer. Strain and let the barley drain off for 30 minutes. Place the barley in a steamer—not all of it—only to a thickness of 2 inches. It will take some time to steam all of the barley. Cook over a high flame for 1½ hours until the color of the grain becomes somewhat transparent and feels rubbery. Be sure to add more water to the steamer during this process, as it will boil off.

Spread out the steamed barley in a large bowl until it cools to body temperature. When the barley cools, place it in a larger bowl and mix in the 7 cups of koji; mix this thoroughly. After the second batch of steamed barley is cooled, add this to the barley that was already mixed with the koji; mix this second batch thoroughly with the first. Repeat this process until all the barley is mixed with the koji and it is all in one large bowl.

11 p.m. In a koji box, spread out this mixture to a 1-inch thickness. In summer, just cover the boxes with a sheet and be sure that a temperature of 80-90 degrees is maintained in the room. In winter, cover the boxes with a sheet, then a bedspread, and place them near the heater. Maintain a temperature of at least 75 degrees in the room. Also, place a pot of water on a hot plate right next to the boxes and keep it going all night, so that the steam from the pot keeps the mixture warm and moist. About 13-16 hours later (1 p.m. next day), look at the mixture in each box. Each should be slightly white to indicate that the koji is working; also, the barley will stick to the boxes. With a wooden spoon or spatula, turn the mixture over so that the top is on

the bottom and vice-versa.

Five hours later (6 p.m.), check to see if the mixture feels warm. Cover again and steam heat overnight, keep maintaining a 75 degree temperature. In the morning (6 a.m.), remove from steam and heat. At 1 p.m., take off the covers; the koji will be gray and look moldy, it will also smell very sweet and feel somewhat powdery when you touch it. Take the barley mixture out of the boxes and put all of it in one pot. You don't want the grain to ferment any more so add 7 cups of salt and mix it in thoroughly and set aside.

Wash the soybeans and soak in twice the amount of water overnight. Bring to a boil on a high flame, remove cover, and cook for 5 hours, adding water as needed. Strain off excess water and save. Let the beans cool. Then place them in a heavy cotton bag. Wearing heavy socks, step on the soybeans and mash them with the weight of your body. In a 20 gallon crock, first sprinkle the bottom with 2 cups of salt, then add mashed soybean barley koji, salt—approximately 7 cups—and leftover water from cooking soybeans. Repeat this procedure one more time. Then mix all in layers together; if it is too hard to mix, add more water (cooled, boiled water) to make it easier to mix. Gently mix until everything is thoroughly blended. Add 2 cups more salt on top. Cover with cellophane paper and place about 7 small stones on top in various places to create pressure. Cover with a cotton cloth, then with a clay or wooden top. Let it sit for 2 years. If you want this miso ready sooner, mix in 10 percent already made miso, about 10 pounds. You can eat this miso 1 year later since fermentation is speeded up. This 1 year miso will have a milder not-so-salty taste.

**Recipes Using Miso
for Warmer Times**

Onion Miso (serves 5)

> 10 small whole onions
> 3 Tbsp miso
> 1 Tbsp oil
> 1-2 cups cold water

Sauté the onions in oil for at least five minutes. Cover with water, bring to a boil, and cook over a low flame for one hour. After the onions have cooled, quarter them about ⅔ of the way down towards the root, so that the onion opens like a flower. Dissolve the miso in a little of the onion juice left over from cooking and add to remaining juice. Cook until it is a thick and creamy consistency and serve it as a sauce over the onions. Allow two onions per serving.

	Protein grams	Methionine/Cystine grams
10 small whole onions	5.2	0.043
3 Tbsp miso	2.9	0.243
Total	8.1	0.286
MDR per serving		4.4%

Carrot and Onion Miso

    3 medium size onions, minced
    1 Tbsp oil
    1 carrot, minced
    ½ Tbsp salt
    2 Tbsp miso

Sauté onions in oil until golden, add carrots, and sauté briefly. Add ½ cup water and salt and cook about fifteen minutes covered. Add miso and continue cooking uncovered over a low flame for another 10 minutes or until much of the liquid has boiled off.

	Protein grams	Methionine/Cystine grams
3 onions	3.0	0.030
1 carrot	.6	0.005
2 Tbsp miso	6.8	0.162
Total	10.4	0.197
MDR		18%

Miso Soup—for older people and children

    1" piece of daikon,* 1½" in diameter, cut sengiri
       (see pg. 140)
    5 scallions, cut in ¼" lengths
    2-3 strips of wakame, cut in small pieces
    1 tsp sesame oil
    2 Tbsp miso

Heat oil, sauté daikon until slightly softened. Add five cups water, bring to a boil, add wakame, and cook until the wakame is soft. Add scallions, bring to a boil, then turn off. Put the miso into a metal strainer and mash it through into the soup; whatever won't go through the strainer, turn over into the soup. Serve immediately.

* long white radish sold mostly in Asian markets

	Protein grams	Methionine/Cystine grams
5 scallions	2.4	0.022
2 Tbsp miso	6.8	0.162
2-3 strips of wakame	3.2	0.095
Total	12.4	0.279
MDR		25%

Soybean Miso (serves 6)

> 2 cups dry soybeans
> 2 Tbsp sesame oil
> ½ cup miso

Heat oil and sauté soybeans over medium flame until golden brown color. Add miso and continue sautéing until miso has a fragrant smell.

	Protein grams	Methionine/Cystine grams
2 cups soybeans	137.2	3.64
½ cup miso	15.0	0.32
Total	152.2	3.96
MDR per serving		10%

Vegetables with Miso Sauce (serves 10)

> 1 eggplant (medium) sliced into ⅓" thick slices, 1" wide, tanzaku (see pg. 141), and deep fried until slightly brown
> 2 carrots, ¼" thick, hasugiri (see pg. 140), deep fried until tender
> 2 cucumbers, cut into ½" thick slices, toss and mix with 2 tsp salt
> 2 zucchini squash, cut in 1" thick slices, cook with ½ tsp salt in a small amount of water
> 1 handful of green vegetable ohitashi,* 2" long

Arrange all vegetables on a big plate. Serve with sesame miso made in the following way:

> 1 cup white sesame seeds
> ½ cup mugi miso

After roasting sesame seeds, grind strongly. Add miso and a little bit (3 tablespoons) of water left from cooking zucchini and grind well (until creamy). Serve with the cooked vegetables.

* Vegetable ohitashi—Bring to a boil 8-10 cups of water. After boiling, add 2 heaping teaspoons salt. Take off cover. Then place 1 bunch of spinach in the pot standing on end. Then bring to a boil over high flame, turn over, and wait until it boils again. When the stem is soft it

is done. Remove to a strainer with leaves hanging over the edge and cool. Repeat with the second bunch. When they are cool, squeeze out excess water and take off pink roots and save for miso soup. Slice spinach straight across in 1"-wide strips. Put these in a bowl, add soy sauce, and mix well. Decorate with bonita flakes. This method is simple and good for any green such as mustard, swiss chard, celery, asparagus, Chinese cabbage, and watercress. After roasting white sesame seeds, chop them with a knife and sprinkle over spinach.

	Protein grams	Methionine/Cystine grams
1 cup sesame seeds	76	4.40
½ cup mugi miso	15	0.32
1 eggplant		0.01
2 carrots		0.005
2 cucumbers		0.006
½ cup mustard green		0.022
Total	91	4.76
MDR per serving (approximately 3 pieces)		43.2%

Vegetable Miso I

> 1 Tbsp oil
> 2 onions, cut in 6 sections
> 4 leaves cabbage, sliced
> 1 carrot, sliced
> ½ tsp salt
> 1 Tbsp miso

Sauté onions, then cabbage, then carrot. Add 1½ cups water and salt and cook 10 minutes. Add miso and cook another 10-15 minutes.

	Protein grams	Methionine/Cystine grams
2 onions	2.8	0.020
4 leaves cabbage	1.4	0.041
1 carrot	1.2	0.039
1 Tbsp miso	2.1	0.045
Total	7.5	0.145
MDR		13%

Vegetable Miso II

½ cup burdock, sasagaki (shaved pencil style, see
  pg. 141)
1 cup onion mawashigiri (see pg. 141)
½ cup squash (any kind) cut in ½" sainome (see pg.
  140)
¼ cup carrot hasugiri (see pg. 140)
¼ cup fresh shiso leaves cut sengiri (see pg. 140) if
  you can get them, otherwise don't worry about it
¼-⅓ cup mugi miso
2 Tbsp sesame oil

Heat pan. Sauté burdock until aroma is gone, add onion, and sauté until color is transparent. Add squash, carrot, and shiso leaves. Add ¼ cup water, bring to a boil, and cook until tender. Add 3 tablespoons of water to the miso and mix well. Add to cooking vegetables. Slowly, carefully mix in the miso. Then bring to a boil until miso aroma is gone. These miso vegetables can be served either hot or cold. If you use more onion, it will taste sweeter. Some children don't like miso soup, though they need miso. So this is an appetizing way of serving it.

	Protein grams	Methionine/Cystine grams
1 cup onion		0.032
½ cup squash		0.024
¼ cup carrot		0.005
¼ cup mugi miso	7.0	0.15
Total	7.0	0.211
MDR		19%

Green Pepper with Miso (serves 2)

> 1 green pepper
> ½ Tbsp mugi miso
> 3 Tbsp soup stock
> ½ Tbsp oil

Cut the pepper in half lengthwise and remove the seeds. Cut each half into 3 pieces likewise. Dilute the miso with the soup stock. Heat up a frying pan. Add oil and sauté the green pepper until the color changes. Then add the diluted miso, cooking for five minutes more. Serve.

	Protein grams	Methionine/Cystine grams
1 green pepper		0.016
½ Tbsp	1.5	0.040
Total	1.5	0.056
MDR per serving		2.5%

Deep Fried Miso Balls

> ½-¾ cup water
> 1 onion, minced
> 1 Tbsp miso
> ⅛ tsp salt
> 1 cup whole wheat flour

Add water to onion and miso, then add flour mixture. Add salt to flour and mix well. The dough should be fairly dry. Drop by spoonfuls into deep oil until they turn a dark golden color. Drain in a strainer, then lay on a platter covered with absorbent paper to take off the excess oil.

	Protein grams	Methionine/Cystine grams
1 cup whole wheat flour	16.0	0.590
1 onion		0.032
1 Tbsp mugi miso	2.9	0.081
Total	18.9	0.703
MDR		12.8%

Pan-Fried Eggplant (serves 1)

> 1 small eggplant
> 1 Tbsp oil
> ¼ tsp mugi miso
> ¼ tsp rice miso
> 2 tsp sake

Remove the head of the eggplant, cut into bite size pieces, soak in plain water for ten minutes, strain off the water. Heat up a frying pan, add the oil, and then the eggplant, and sauté with a cover until the eggplant is tender. Mix the miso and sake. When the eggplant is done, add this miso mixture, bring to a boil, and serve.

	Protein grams	Methionine/Cystine grams
1 small eggplant		0.005
¼ tsp rice miso	0.25	0.007
¼ tsp mugi miso	0.25	0.007
Total	0.50	0.019
MDR		1.7%

Eggplant Salad (serves 5)

> 1 med. eggplant
> 3 Tbsp sesame oil
> 2 tsp soy sauce
> 1 bunch scallions
> ⅔ cup soup stock*
> 2 cucumbers
> 1 tomato
> 1 tsp salt
> ¼ lb mugi miso
> 1 tsp orange rind
> 1 Tbsp bonita flakes

Remove the head of the eggplant and cut it into ¼" rounds. Soak in plain water for ten minutes, then strain. Heat up a fry pan, add the oil, add the eggplant, sauté until it is completely done, and sprinkle with soy sauce. In another pan, combine the soup stock and miso. Bring to a boil. When the miso has a fragrant aroma, cook without a cover and mix in the orange rind. Slice the cucumbers into thin rounds, sprinkle with 1 teaspoon of salt, let sit for 10 minutes. Cut tomato into ¼" half-moons. Cook scallions in salted boiling water for a few minutes, until they are soft, then cut into 1" lengths. Place the scallions on the bottom of the serving bowl, then the eggplant and miso. Sprinkle with bonita flakes. Arrange cucumbers and to-mato around eggplant.

*Soup stock—Left over chicken or fish bones

        1 bone
        7 cups water
        1 tsp salt
        ¼ tsp pepper

	Protein grams	Methionine/Cystine grams
1 med. eggplant		0.007
1 bunch scallions		0.006
2 cucumbers		0.006
1 tomato		0.008
¼ lb mugi miso	14.0	0.310
1 Tbsp bonita flakes	14.0	0.199
2 tsp soy sauce	1.1	0.017
Total	29.1	0.553
MDR per serving		2%

Eggplant with Sesame Butter

        10 small eggplants
        2 Tbsp white sesame seeds
        3 Tbsp soy sauce

Remove the head of the eggplant. Remove the skin with a potato peeler. Cook the whole eggplants in salted boiling water until they are soft. Strain off the water. Place the eggplants on a cutting board, put another cutting board on top of them and press so that the excess water is drained off. Tear each eggplant into 4 pieces lengthwise with your hands. Roast the sesame seeds (see below), put them in a suribachi with the soy sauce, and grind for ten minutes. Add egg-plant to the suribachi and mix well with the sesame seeds.

	Protein grams	Methionine/Cystine grams
10 small eggplants		0.050
2 Tbsp sesame seeds	9.5	0.550
3 Tbsp soy sauce	3.6	0.120
Total	13.1	0.720
MDR		60%

Roasting sesame seeds—If you roast too much or too little, the taste is not good. It is very important not to roast unevenly. To avoid this, roast on a medium flame, stirring constantly until all seeds are equally roasted. A very high or very low flame is not good for roasting evenly. White sesame seeds and brown sesame seeds become very fragrant and taste good when roasted dark. Black sesame seeds are more yang, thus over-roasting makes them taste bitter. Roast the sesame seeds until your thumb and fourth finger can crush the seeds (your other fingers are too strong to test). When the roasted seeds crush easily, they are done. Another test is to eat a few of the roasted seeds. Raw seeds have a green taste, which means they are not done. If they have a good taste, they are done. Sesame seeds are most important in our daily food. So, please cook them with your whole heart. If you cannot make good sesame salt or good rice, you are not yet a good macrobiotic cook. Although cooking rice and preparing sesame salt are simple, they are the most important part of a macrobiotic diet.

Split Pea Miso Soup (serves 10)

    2 cups split peas
    1 tsp fish shavings (optional)
    2 large onions
    2 Tbsp rice flour
    1 cup chopped celery
    ⅓-½ cup mugi miso
    1 cup chopped carrots
    1 Tbsp oil

Wash split peas and soak in 4 cups of water overnight. Boil in 8 cups of water with strips of kombu and split peas until tender. Remove kombu; sauté onions, fish shavings, celery, and carrots in oil; add soup to flour, then put in with rest of soup. (Mix some of soup in blender if creamy style is preferred.) Add miso to taste.

	Protein grams	Methionine/Cystine grams
2 cups split peas	96.0	2.448
2 large onions	4.0	0.040
1 cup chopped celery	0.4	0.005
1 cup carrots	1.2	0.010
1 tsp fish shavings	2.4	0.070
2 Tbsp rice flour	2.0	0.067
⅓ cup mugi miso	27.5	0.319
Total	133.5	2.959
MDR per serving		27%

Recipes Using Miso for Colder Times

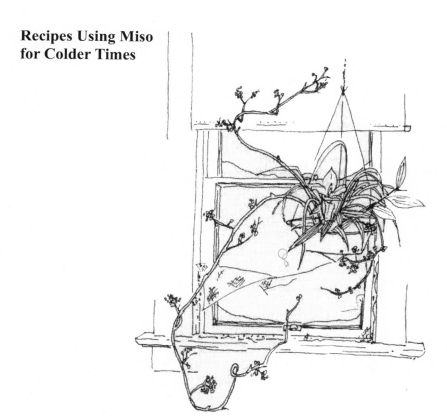

Mushroom Gravy for Pasta

> 2 onions
> ½ Tbsp oil
> 3 cloves garlic
> bay leaf
> ½ lb fresh mushrooms
> about 2 Tbsp miso
> 1 tsp salt
> several crookneck squash or zucchini

Sauté chopped onions in oil, add whole garlic cloves, then sliced mushrooms, then chopped squash. When browned, add seasonings, salt, and small amount of water. Simmer until cooked—remove garlic. Add miso and let stand a few minutes. Serve over spaghetti.

	Protein grams	Methionine/Cystine grams
2 onions	2.0	0.020
½ lb mushroom	9.2	0.367
½ lb squash	1.4	0.018
2 Tbsp miso	3.4	0.162
Total	16.0	0.567
MDR		50%

Country Soup with Chicken (serves 5)

> 1 lb chicken with bone
> 1 carrot, cut rangiri (see pg. 139)
> 1 lb albi or taro
> 6" daikon
> 1 scallion, ⅓" koguchi-cut (see pg. 139)
> 5 medium shiitake, soak in water
> ⅓ cup miso (½ barley miso & ½ rice miso or ⅓ cup
>   barley miso only)
> 8 cups water

Bring water to a boil and add the chicken. When marrow and potassium come out of the bone, skim it off and discard it but leave the chicken and bone in the pot. Continue cooking at low-boil for fifty minutes. Add the vegetables and cook until tender. Dilute the miso and add to the soup. Cook ten minutes longer until vegetables absorb the miso taste. Add the scallion and bring to a boil. Remove from stove and serve. Adding more of a variety of vegetables, selected with a balance of both yin and yang, increases the flavor and richness of this soup.

The secret of this recipe is the long cooking time, which makes the chicken tender and tasty as well as the blending of the miso with the vegetables.

	Protein gm.	Methionine/Cystine gm.
1 lb chicken	91.0	3.695
1 lb albi	8.6	0.095
1 scallion	0.3	0.003
5 shiitake	0.7	0.020
⅓ cup miso	11.4	0.240
Total	112.0	4.054
MDR per serving		14.6%

Kenchin Soup (serves 5)

> 4" daikon, sliced in five pieces
> 1 carrot, cut hangetsu (see pg. 140)
> 1 lb albi, remove the skin, cut rangiri (see pg. 139)
> 1 block tofu (squeeze out excess water by pressing between two cutting boards, covered with a cotton cloth), cut ½" thick and 1" squares and deep fry.
> 2 Tbsp miso
> ½ tsp salt
> ½ lb sake-no-kasu,* dissolved in hot water or cut into small pieces
> 2 Tbsp oil
> 5 scallions, cut in ¼" lengths

Sauté the scallions, daikon, albi, carrot, and fried tofu in that order, add 6 cups water, and bring to a boil. When the vegetables are half done, add the sake-no-kasu and cook for 10 minutes. Add the miso and cook an additional 5 minutes. Add more salt if necessary. Sprinkle with orange rind and serve.

* Sake-no-kasu is a residue of making rice wine and can be bought at a Japanese market in any large town.

	Protein grams	Methionine/Cystine grams
4" daikon (white radish)	0.6	0.001
1 carrot	0.6	0.020
1 lb albi	9.0	0.095
1 block tofu	12.0	0.300
2 Tbsp miso	4.3	0.090
5 scallion	2.4	0.022
Total	28.5	0.528
MDR per serving		1.8%

Country Soup with Salmon Head (serves 5)

> ½ salmon head (fresh, not salty)
> 2 daikon, cut ½ moon pieces ⅓" thick
> 1 onion, minced
> 1 Tbsp oil
> miso
> water

Chop salmon, sauté in 1 tablespoon oil. When color changes, add the minced onion and daikon, then water to cover 1" above vegetables. Cook (boil) on medium flame until tender. Add miso. It is good to cool this completely. Then reheat on stove for best flavor just before serving.

	Protein grams	Methionine/Cystine grams
½ salmon head	17.0	0.741
2 daikon (white radish)	2.0	0.004
1 onion	2.0	0.022
3 Tbsp	6.3	0.135
Total	27.3	0.902
By serving five, one will get:		
	5.4	0.180
MDR per serving		3.2%

Radish-Turnip Nabe

1 daikon, 4" x 1½", cut lengthwise in half, then ⅓" thick koguchigiri (see pg. 139), boil in salt water until tender

5 turnips, cut ⅓" mawashigiri (see pg. 141), cook in salt water

5 Chinese cabbage leaves, boiled in salt water for a few minutes; stack leaves end to tip on a sushi mat, roll up, and cut into 1½" rolls.

1 bu. scallions, cut hasugiri (see pg. 140)

2 heaping Tbsp mugi miso

⅛" piece dashi kombu, cut part way through every 1"

Around the edge of an 8" shallow pan, make a bank of miso against the sides. Pour three cups of water into the pan gently so as not to disturb the miso, turn the flame to high, add kombu, and bring to a boil. Then gently place each vegetable in a separate section; daikon, cabbage, turnip, and scallion. Bring to a boil and cook for ten minutes. The miso slowly dissolves into the vegetables as they stew and gives them a wonderful flavor. If possible, bring the pan to the table and cook with a heating unit. Serve with toasted mochi, boiled noodles, or soba. These are nice to add, especially if you have left-over juice. This dish is good for the cold season because it makes your body warm very quickly.

	Protein grams	Methionine/Cystine grams
5 turnips	2.9	0.097
5 Chinese cabbage leaves	1.4	0.041
1 bu. scallions	2.4	0.022
2 Tbsp mugi miso	4.3	0.090
Total	11.0	0.250
MDR		22%

CHAPTER 3

Traditional Soy Sauce

The most important seasoning, next to salt and miso, is traditional soy sauce, even for Americans. The average Japanese person gets 18 percent of total protein from soybean products such as miso, soy sauce, tofu, and natto. Rice gives 30 percent of protein and fish supplies 20 percent.

It is not an exaggeration to say that Japanese and Chinese cooking depends on soy sauce. It is soy sauce that makes Japanese and Chinese cuisines so delicious.

In Japanese cuisine, soy sauce is used as a seasoning in cooking, as an ingredient in marinades, and as a dip. The August 1960 issue of *House Beautiful* reported that Japanese cooking was the most delicious cuisine their researchers tasted in their world-wide trip spent experiencing different cuisines. It says, "Another basic requirement for Japanese cooking is the dipping sauces, all of which revolve around soy sauce. There are four fine ones: soy sauce and lemon juice (half and half) garnished with finely chopped scallion, soy sauce with grated white radish, soy sauce with grated fresh ginger, and soy sauce garnished with flakes of dried bonita. Individual servings of dipping sauces are provided to each person, so you can adjust how much sauce you get on each bit, seasoning up or down at will."

1. History

Soy sauce has a history that is centuries old. In ancient times, making soy sauce was a household industry in China. Descriptions of the process are found in books written more than 1,500 years ago.

In ancient times, Japanese soy sauce was made with animal protein as a source of inosinic acid. One scholar says that the modern soy sauce processed by fermentation of soybeans and wheat with the help of bacteria was imported from China to Japan around 754 A.D. However, there are several who dispute this. According to I. Kajiura, author of *The Secret of Zen Cooking*, the first book that mentioned the use of soy sauce in Japan was the *Shi-Jo School Cookbook*, written in 1489. In this book, soy sauce was called "tamari miso." Tamari is the liquid that drips to the bottom of a miso keg while miso is aging. (Tamari literally means *a liquid drip*.) Therefore, tamari is the original form of soy sauce in Japan, but it was made from miso, a fermented product of soybeans and barley. Tamari is no longer a miso by-product, but soy sauce, which is made from fermented soybeans and wheat, instead of barley or rice.

In the 1970s in America, the name "tamari" is used as the trade name for the traditional soy sauce exclusively approved by the Japanese macrobiotic food distributors in Osaka and Tokyo. The Tokyo distributors recently introduced Lima soy sauce because of the increased demand for quality soy sauce in America. Named after Mrs. Lima Ohsawa, it is manufactured to meet her specific requirements. Lima soy sauce is the same, or of even better quality, than tamari soy sauce.

Japanese soy sauce was authentic and a family industry until the beginning of the 20th Century. But with the importation of machinery, the soy sauce industry developed rapidly and changed the process to mass production with the use of chemicals such as hydrochloric acid. Furthermore, most modern Japanese soy sauces use sugar in order to "improve" the taste and shorten the period of aging. MSG (monosodium glutamate) is another chemical that increased soy sauce production and reduced its quality.

George Ohsawa, the founder of the macrobiotic diet in America, was aware of the fact that modern commercialism would confuse the consumer if authentic soy sauce and commercial soy sauce were sold with the same name, so he named the authentic soy sauce "tamari" in Europe and America when he introduced the macrobiotic diet into these countries.

[The use of the word "tamari" and the phrase "tamari soy sauce" in the 1970s has caused much confusion over the years.

Thus, we have changed "tamari" to "soy sauce" and "tamari soy sauce" to "traditional soy sauce" in the remainder of this book. Ed.]

2. Chemical Change of Traditional Soy Sauce

The chemical changes involved in the production of soy sauce are complex and inter-related. Wheat serves as a carbohydrate source for the growth of the micro-organisms. The mold supplies the enzymes necessary to convert starch into sugar, which in turn is acted upon by all three micro-organisms. The mold and yeast produce some alcohol from the sugar. The bacteria produce lactic acid and other organic acids. Esters, such as ethyl acetates, are also formed by inter-action of the alcohol and organic acids. They account for much of the aroma and flavor of the sauce. Other important flavor constituents are amino acids. The salt quantity (approximately 18 percent) serves to neutralize the production of the acids. The amino acids are produced by enzymatic decomposition of the proteins in the soybeans and wheat. Most of the protein degradation (breakdown in amino acids) and carbohydrate fermentation occurs during the first weeks of prime fermentation. After this time, the flavor matures by very slow reactions that involve the formation of esters and the splitting of dextrins.

It is not necessary to add coloring to traditional soy sauce as is done to most commercial brands of soy sauce because of the long aging period that gives it a deep rich color. However, since soy sauce is a product of nature with its constantly changing conditions, the color of soy sauce will vary slightly from one batch to another. The color differences in traditional soy sauce are rather a manifestation of the natural product instead of a sign of disorderliness or incompleteness. This difference in color is the sign of its natural identity.

3. How to Make Traditional Soy Sauce

Production of traditional soy sauce is much more delicate than the production of miso.

5½ lbs soybeans

4½ lbs wheat
5 lbs salt
15 lbs water

Wash soybeans and soak in water for several hours. Boil with water to soften and then cool to room temperature. Wash wheat, and roast after rinsing. Then crack it.

Mix cooked soybeans, cracked wheat, and Koji bactteria. (Aspergillus Aryzae and Aspergillus Soya are usually used in Koji bacteria.) The quality of traditional soy sauce depends, to a large extent, on this process. The ingredients should then be well mixed, placed in shallow wooden trays, and kept in the Koji room, where the temperature should not go below 91° F.

After six hours, the room temperature will begin to rise. The temperature must be watched closely so that it will not rise higher than 104° F.

About seventy hours later, take out the mixture.

Make a salt solution in the following proportions: Mix five pounds of salt with seven quarts of water, which will make the solution's approximate specific gravity 1:17.

Put the soybeans and wheat mixture in a keg and add the salt solution to it. The keg can be made of wood or porcelain. In order to absorb more oxygen for the growth of bacteria, the mixture must be mixed every day for about one month.

After aging about eighteen months or more, place the mixture in a cloth and squeeze out the juice. The juice that comes out is traditional soy sauce, and the residue is called "moromi," a very nutritious food.

4. How to Use Traditional Soy Sauce

a) Scallion Dip

Combine soy sauce and bonita flakes. Add to Dashi broth, which is usually made by boiling kombu in a saucepan (see *Do of Cooking* or other macrobiotic cookbook). Bring to a boil on a low flame. Remove from heat and let cool. Mince scallions.

Serve sauce in individual small dishes for dipping and serve scallions in a small bowl. Bonita flakes are optional.

This is good for noodles, especially for buckwheat noodles.

b) Radish Dip

Combine soy sauce, grated radish, and Dashi broth in a saucepan. Bring to boil on a low flame. Remove from heat and let cool. Serve sauce in individual small dishes for dipping.

This is good for tempura (deep fried vegetables, shrimp, or fish).

c) Ginger Soy Sauce

Add grated ginger to soy sauce. This is good with fish.

d) Green Peas and Shrimp Nishime (serves 5)

> 1 lb fresh green peas
> 1 1b. shrimp, cleaned and de-veined (allow two per person)
> 3½ cups soup stock
> 1½ Tbsp soy sauce
> 1½ tsp salt
> 1 Tbsp arrowroot flour, dissolved in 2 Tbsp water

Bring soup stock to a boil, add peas, cook uncovered until half done. Add soy sauce and salt, then add shrimp when peas are almost done. Do not cook too long. Bring all these to a boil, add dissolved arrowroot flour, and bring to boil again until thickened and transparent. Serve in a deep bowl.

Soy Sauce Cooking
for Warmer Times

Nori with Soy Sauce

> 1 pkg. nori seaweed
> 2 cups water
> 3 Tbsp soy sauce

Break nori into 1" squares. Soak in water for twenty minutes. Cook in the same water for thirty minutes in a covered sauce pan. The water should be all absorbed. Add traditional soy sauce, cover, and simmer thirty minutes longer. Stored in refrigerator, this will keep for a week or more.

	Protein grams	Methionine/Cystine grams
1 pkg. nori	34.2	1.63
3 Tbsp soy sauce	5.7	0.12
Total	39.9	1.75
MDR		150%

Buckwheat Noodles with Sesame Sauce

> 8 oz buckwheat noodles*
> 8 cups soup stock
> 2 heaping Tbsp sesame butter
> 5 Tbsp soy sauce
> 1 bunch scallions, sarashi-negi**
> 2 sheets nori, roasted and crushed

Mix the sesame butter with 1 cup of soup stock, add 2 tablespoons of soy sauce. If the noodles are cold, put them into hot water to warm them and place in serving bowls. Bring the soup stock to a boil, add 3 tablespoons soy sauce. Over the noodles pour some sesame butter sauce, then the soup stock, then nori and scallions sarashi-negi; or the sesame sauce, nori, and scallions sarashi-negi can be put on the table and the individual can serve himself according to his taste.

*To make buckwheat noodles: Bring 8 cups of water to a boil and add the soba noodles. Bring to a boil again. Add 1 cup of cold water and bring to a boil again. Shut off heat and let sit for a minute. Then strain the buckwheat noodles and rinse quickly with cold water until noodles are completely cold. After about two minutes, when noodles are thoroughly drained, place them on a clean cotton towel in strips about 1½" wide and ½" thick to drain more.

** Sarashi-negi means "water-washed scallion." To prepare this condiment, chop scallions into very thin pieces, then cover with cotton cloth and twist. Bring to the sink and wash with cold water, rubbing firmly with the fingers. Then squeeze scallion to take out the green color. Repeat the washing one more time.

	Protein grams	Methionine/Cystine grams
8 oz buckwheat noodles	27.0	0.412
2 Tbsp sesame butter	9.5	0.055
5 Tbsp soy sauce	9.5	0.200
1 bunch scallion	2.4	0.022
Total	48.4	0.689
MDR		62%

Bean Thread Noodle Gratin (serves 10)

½ small bag bean thread noodles
1 tsp salt
10 rounds of dry wheat gluten
2 tsp soy sauce
1 medium onion, sengiri (see pg. 140)
2 Tbsp whole wheat pastry flour
½ small carrot, sengiri (see pg. 140)
1 cup soup stock
1 Tbsp minced parsley
2 Tbsp oil

Bring 8 cups of salted water to a boil. Add bean thread noodles and cook 5 minutes with cover on. Let noodles stand 30 minutes. Drain and cut into 2-inch pieces.

Soak dry wheat gluten for 5 minutes in 1 cup of cold water. Drain gluten and put into a cup of boiling soup stock to which has been added ¼ teaspoon salt and 2 teaspoons soy sauce. Boil about 10 minutes.

Sauté onion and carrot in oil and simmer in soup stock 20 minutes. Thicken sauce with whole wheat pastry flour and season with salt, parsley, and soy sauce. Simmer a few minutes longer.

Place Noodle Gratin in two layers in casserole with sauce in between and then on top. Bake in covered casserole in 350 degree oven until sauce bubbles on top—about 20 minutes.

	Protein grams	Methionine/Cystine grams
½ small bag bean noodles*	24.4	.417
10 round gluten (2 lbs)	376.0	14.637
1 onion (100 gm.)	1.4	0.10
½ carrot (50 gm.)	0.6	0.19
2 Tbsp w.w. pastry flour (28.3 gm.)	3.4	.145
2 tsp soy sauce (9.4 gm.)	0.7	0.12
Total	406.5	15.240
MDR per serving		11%

* These values are for 3½ oz mung beans (100 gm.)

Ohitashi (serves 5)

2 bunches spinach (approximately)
2 oz bonita flakes
8-10 cups water
2 tsp white sesame seeds
1½ tsp soy sauce

Bring to a boil 8-10 cups of water. After boiling add 2 heaping tea-spoons salt. Take off cover. Then place 1 bunch of spinach in the pot standing on end. Then bring to a boil over high flame, turn over, and wait until it boils again. When the stem is soft, it is done. Remove to a strainer with leaves hanging over the edge and cool. Repeat with the second bunch. When they are cool, squeeze out excess water and take off pink roots and save for miso soup. Slice spinach straight across in 1" wide strips. Then put these in a bowl, add soy sauce, and mix well. Decorate with bonita flakes. This method is simple and good for any green such as mustard, swiss chard, celery, asparagus, Chinese cabbage, and watercress. After roasting white sesame seeds, chop them with a knife and sprinkle over spinach.

	Protein grams	Methionine/Cystine grams
2 bunches spinach	2.3	0.085
1½ tsp soy sauce	0.5	0.009
2 tsp white sesame seeds	3.2	0.183
2 oz bonita flakes*	40.0	1.740
Total	46.0	2.017
MDR per serving		7.32%

* The value of bonita flakes is taken from the value of dried cod.

Soybean Surprise (serves 6)

> 2 cups soybeans
> 5-6 cups water
> 2 cups onions, minced
> 1 cup carrots, minced
> Parsley, minced
> **Sauce**
> 4 Tbsp tahini
> 4 Tbsp water
> Miso to taste (about 1 Tbsp)
> Green scallions (Optional)

Soak soybeans for 6 hours or overnight. Place in pressure cooker, bring to full pressure, reduce flame, and cook for forty-five minutes. Watch soybeans so that liquid does not clog air vent. Sauté onions and carrots. Place tahini and water in a saucepan, stir constantly while cooking on a medium flame until they have a creamy consistency. Add onions and carrots and simmer 10-15 minutes until flavors mingle. Blend in miso until desired taste is obtained. May need to add a little more water for desired consistency. When using scallions, add them to the sauce just before serving, so that they are heated through but not well cooked. Place soybeans in serving bowls, pour sauce over, and sprinkle parsley on top.

	Protein grams	Methionine/Cystine grams
2 cups soybeans	158.4	1.720
2 cups onions	2.8	0.026
1 cup carrot	0.6	0.019
4 Tbsp soy sauce	19.2	1.100
1 Tbsp miso	2.0	0.041
Total	183.0	2.906
MDR per serving		7.33%

Buffalo Stew

> 1 cup whole hard corn
> Sage (optional)
> 1 cup beans
> 2 Tbsp seitan
> 1½ cups assorted vegetables (onion and carrot)
> 2 Tbsp soy sauce
> Water

Soak the corn for 24 hours, then put it in a heavy pot with 3 cups of water and a piece of kombu. Bring to a boil, place a heat diffuser under pot, and simmer very low overnight. Soak the beans (pinto, navy, kidney—whatever kind you choose) overnight and cook by themselves in 2½ cups water until tender but firm.

Vegetables to use can vary—any root vegetable (carrots, parsnips, onions, burdock), also green pepper, winter squash, anything that will hold up fairly well. Cut these into small chunks. They can be sautéed first or added to the corn raw and simmered.

	Protein grams	Methionine/Cystine grams
1 cup whole corn	7.8	0.246
1 cup beans	23.0	0.460
1½ cups onion & carrot	0.9	0.029
2 Tbsp seitan	12.1	0.248
2 Tbsp soy sauce	3.8	0.080
Total	47.5	1.063
MDR		100%

Udon with Soy Sauce

½ cup azuki beans
1½ cups water
1¾ tsp salt
1 bunch scallions, chopped
1 tsp oil
2½ tsp soy sauce
1 lb udon noodles

Cook the azuki beans in 2½ to 3 times the amount of water for pressure cooker; use 4 times the amount of water for regular cooking.

Pressure cooking: Place beans and water in pressure cooker. Bring to full pressure and cook 45 minutes. Allow pressure to reduce to normal. Remove cover, add salt and soy sauce, and cook slowly until liquid boils off. Adjust seasoning to taste.

Regular cooking: Brine to boil and cook on very low flame for about 2 hours. Remove cover, add salt, and continue to cook without cover on low flame until liquid boils off.

Open cooker and add ½ teaspoon salt. Reserve.

Sauté scallions in oil over high flame, stirring constantly. Lower flame and add ¼ teaspoon salt and soy sauce. Cook for five minutes. Reserve. Cook udon with 1 teaspoon salt. Drain and mix all ingredients together in a pot. Serve warm in winter or in the summer put in a square pan and refrigerate. Cut into squares and serve.

	Protein grams	Methionine/Cystine grams
½ cup azuki	23.0	0.332
1 bunch scallions	2.4	0.022
2½ tsp soy sauce	1.3	0.027
1 lb udon noodles	55.2	1.980
Total	81.9	2.361
MDR		200%

Wakame Cucumber Sesame Salad

> 2 cucumbers, rangiri (see pg. 139; if waxed, re-
> move outer skin)
> 1 Tbsp sesame butter
> 1 tsp soy sauce
> ⅓ cup wakame, soaked in water for 20 minutes,
> washed and cut into ½" lengths

Mix 1 teaspoon salt with the cucumbers. Keep under slight pressure for 10 minutes (use a bowl with water and place it over the cucumbers to create pressure). Squeeze out the excess water and mix the cucumbers with the wakame. Mix the sesame butter and soy sauce thoroughly. If the sauce is too thick, add a little more water to make it creamy. Mix in the cucumber and wakame.

	Protein grams	Methionine/Cystine grams
2 cucumbers	0.7	0.007
⅓ cup wakame	1.3	0.058
1 Tbsp sesame butter	9.5	0.550
1 tsp soy sauce	0.6	0.013
Total	12.1	0.608
MDR		55.2%

Scallop Cucumber Sauce (serves 6)

> 20 scallops (1 lb)
> 2 Tbsp kuzu arrowroot, diluted in a little water
> 1½ cucumbers, sliced thin in rounds
> 1 Tbsp oil
> 4 cups water—use scallop cooking water
> 4 tsp soy sauce
> ½ tsp salt

Sauté cucumber in oil. Boil scallops about three minutes. Drain, reserving liquid for sauce. Add scallop juice and water to cucumbers (to make up the four cups) and boil about 15 minutes. Add salt and soy sauce. Boil five minutes longer. Add kuzu arrowroot. Boil a few minutes longer, adding scallops last. (If cooked too long, scallops become tough.) Serve over rice.

	Protein grams	Methionine/Cystine grams
20 scallops (1 lb)	84.15	3.582
1½ cucumbers	0.7	0.007
2 Tbsp arrowroot		
4 tsp soy sauce	2.4	0.050
Total	84.40	3.639
MDR per serving		9%

Tahini-Soy Sauce

> 1 Tbsp tahini
> 1 onion, minced
> 3 Tbsp soy sauce
> 1 tsp corn oil
> 1 cup water

Sauté onion in oil until transparent. Add water. Cover and simmer about 20 minutes. Add tahini and soy sauce, cover and cook five minutes.

	Protein grams	Methionine/Cystine grams
1 Tbsp tahini	4.8	0.28
3 Tbsp soy sauce	2.9	0.05
1 onion	1.4	0.01
Total	9.1	0.33
MDR		30%

Onion Sauce

    1 med. onion, sliced thin
    1 cup water
    2 Tbsp oil
    ¼ tsp salt
    2 Tbsp flour—whole wheat, whole wheat pastry, or
        unbleached white
    2 tsp soy sauce

Heat oil. Sauté onions until golden. Blend in flour and continue as for béchamel sauce* (see below). Gradually add cold water stirring constantly. Lower flame and simmer 10 minutes. Add salt and cook 5 minutes. Add soy sauce and simmer a few minutes longer. Delicious served with buckwheat groats or noodles.

* Béchamel sauce can be prepared with either 2 parts flour to 1 part oil, or 3 parts flour to 1 part oil. The former is more delicious, but you may not want to use so much oil in one dish. The amount of water or soup stock used depends upon desired thickness of sauce. Heat the oil slightly and add flour, roasting and stirring gently. Do not roast too long—only until lumps are smoothed out. Color should remain unchanged, with the flour a powdery white. For the best result, cool before adding soup stock or water. Bring to a boil and simmer for 20 minutes, stirring occasionally. Add salt to taste and simmer a few more minutes. Keep hot until serving time or sauce will harden.

	Protein grams	Methionine/Cystine grams
1 med. onion	0.7	0.006
2 Tbsp whole wheat flour	6.6	0.250
2 tsp soy sauce	1.2	0.022
Total	8.5	0.258
MDR		23%

Soy Sauce Cooking for Colder Times

Egg Drop Soup (serves 15)

> 1 onion, chopped
> 1 Tbsp oil
> 1/5 cup chirimen iriko (small dried fish)
> 1½ tsp salt
> 2 Tbsp soy sauce
> ½ bunch raw scallions, chopped
> 9 cups water
> 1 egg beaten, white only

Sauté onion in oil, add the fish, sauté it well, add water, and cook for 20 minutes. Add salt and soy sauce. Bring to a boil and stir in the egg until it is cooked. It will take a few minutes for the egg to harden. Serve with chopped raw scallions.

	Protein grams	Methionine/Cystine grams
1 onion	1.4	0.010
2 Tbsp soy sauce	3.8	0.080
1/5 cup chirimen iriko	16.0	0.696
½ bunch scallion	1.2	0.011
1 egg white	2.7	0.171
Total	25.1	1.219
MDR per serving		7.4%

French Onion Soup

> 3 onions, mawashigiri (see pg. 141), thin
> 4 cups soup stock
> 1 tsp oil
> Salt to taste
> Soy sauce to taste

Sauté the onions in oil. Add the soup stock and cook until done. Season with soy sauce and salt and simmer five minutes longer. Serve over dried bread or with croutons.

Soup Stock

> 3" piece kombu
> ½ tsp salt
> 1 Tbsp bonita flakes
> 1 Tbsp soy sauce
> 6 cups water

Bring 3 cups of water and kombu to a boil, strain and reserve kombu. Add 3 more cups of cold water, bring to another boil, and cook for 30 minutes. Add bonita flakes, bring to a boil, and cook for 1 minute. Remove from the flame and allow bonita flakes to settle; strain and add salt and soy sauce.

	Protein grams	Methionine/Cystine grams
3 onions	4.2	0.030
3" piece kombu	1.8	0.060
1 Tbsp bonita flakes	10.0	0.435
1 Tbsp soy sauce	1.9	0.040
Total	17.9	0.565
MDR		51%

Salmon Country Soup (serves 5)

½ salted salmon head, cut into small pieces
1-10" daikon, cut into pieces ½" long x ⅓" thick
1 carrot, cut into ⅓" half moons
2 medium onions, cut into eight pieces mawashigiri
  (see pg. 141)
3 medium potatoes, cut rangiri (see pg. 139)
3 pieces agé (2" x ½" x ½"), cut in half
5 cups water
1 tsp ginger juice
2 Tbsp soy sauce
1 Tbsp oil

Sauté the salmon head, then add potatoes, onions, daikon and carrots. Sauté well, then add the five cups water. Cook until tender. Add the agé. Taste first before adding salt and soy sauce as needed. Add one teaspoon ginger juice before turning off the flame. Remove from heat and serve immediately.

Any salted fish or other vegetables may be used. (Use albi instead of potatoes for those who are sick.)

	Protein grams	Methionine/Cystine grams
½ salmon head	17.0	0.741
1 10" daikon radish	1.0	0.002
1 carrot	0.6	0.020
2 onions	3.0	0.028
3 potatoes	4.4	0.080
3 agé	1.2	0.032
2 Tbsp soy sauce	1.7	0.080
Total	28.90	0.983
MDR per serving		3.6%

Sake-No-Kasu Soup (serves 6)

¼ lb sake-no-kasu
¼ lb salmon, cut in 1" square pieces
2 agé, cut sengiri (see pg. 140)
1 carrot, cut tanzaku (see pg. 141)
4" daikon which is about 2" in diameter, cut icho-
    giri (see pg. 140)
3 scallions, cut ¼" lengths
1 piece of konnyaku, cut tanzaku

Cut the sake-no-kasu in small pieces, place in a suribachi, and grind with a small amount of water. Bring to a boil six cups water, add the salmon, daikon, carrot, konnyaku, and agé all at the same time, bring to another boil. Skim off the bubbles that form at the top of the soup. When the vegetables begin to soften, add the diluted sake-no-kasu, bring the soup to another boil. Season with 1 teaspon of salt and 1-1½ tablespoon soy sauce. Boil until the vegetables are tender. Add the scallions, remove from the flame, serve immediately.

	Protein grams	Methionine/Cystine grams
¼ lb sake-no-kasu	2.0	0.036
¼ lb salmon	20.0	0.741
2 agé	1.2	0.022
1 carrot	0.6	0.020
4" daikon	0.6	0.001
3 scallions	0.9	0.009
Total	32.1	0.829
MDR per serving		2%

Salmon With Sake-No-Kasu Soup (serves 5)

½ salted salmon head (can use any fish head),
   wash and cut in ½" pieces
½ daikon, cut sasagaki (see pg. 141)
1 scallion, cut on diagonal
4" x 6" piece dashi kombu
½ cup of ¼" sake-no-kasu
soy sauce
albi is also good used in this recipe

Start with 10 cups water. Add the kombu and soak for five hours. Add 1 cup of kombu stock to the sake-no-kasu and cream together. Bring the kombu stock to a boil, add the daikon and salmon-head.

	Protein grams	Methionine/Cystine grams
½ salted salmon head	17.0	0.741
½ daikon	0.6	0.001
1 scallion	0.3	0.003
½ cup sake-no-kasu	6.0	0.108
2 Tbsp soy sauce	1.7	0.080
Total	25.6	0.933
MDR per serving		3.2%

Chicken Ojiya

> 6 cups water or chicken stock
> 1 Tbsp sake
> 1 bu. scallions, cut hasugiri (see pg. 140)
> 1 chicken drumstick, cut into small pieces
> 1 tsp salt
> 1 Tbsp soy sauce
> 3 cups cooked rice
> ½ block tofu, cut ⅓" squares, sainome (see pg. 140)
> 1 heaping Tbsp minced parsley

Bring chicken stock or water to boil, add sake, scallions, chicken and salt, soy sauce, and cold cooked rice. Bring to boil again over high flame, then turn low, and cook for thirty minutes. Shut off flame. Sprinkle with the parsley and serve immediately.

Chicken stock will be made by the following recipe:

> 1 bone (left over chicken or fish bones. Use organi-
>   cally grown chicken.)
> 7 cups water
> 1 tsp salt
> ¼ tsp pepper

	Protein grams	Methionine/Cystine grams
1 bunch scallions	2.4	0.022
1 chicken drumstick	20.6	0.814
1 Tbsp soy sauce	1.9	0.040
3 cups cooked rice	11.1	0.356
½ block tofu	6.0	0.150
Total	42.0	1.382
MDR		125%

Shellfish Ojiya (serves 5)

½ lb shellfish
1 Tbsp soy sauce
1 tsp salt
3 cups cooked rice
6 cups water
1-3" carrot, cut sengiri (see pg. 140)
6" piece dashi kombu
½ lb albi, cut in quarters
1 Tbsp sake—optional
1 bunch watercress

Set shellfish in a strainer into a bowl of salted water, then shake well. Bring to a boil the six cups water with the kombu in a heavy cast iron or stainless steel pot. Just before the water boils, remove the kombu, and add the salt and soy sauce (and the sake if desired) and the shellfish. After it comes to a boil again, remove the shellfish. Add the cooked rice, albi, carrot, and bring to a boil on high flame. Then turn low and cook for forty-five minutes. Add watercress and bring to a boil again. Add the shellfish and turn off the flame. Serve immediately while it is piping hot.

	Protein grams	Methionine/Cystine grams
½ lb shellfish	42.4	1.831
1 Tbsp soy sauce	1.9	0.040
3 cups cooked rice	11.1	0.356
1-3" carrot	1.2	0.040
½ lb albi	4.3	0.047
1 bunch watercress	2.2	0.013
Total	63.1	2.327
MDR per serving		8.4%

Ojiya (Rice Gruel)
How to Make Good Ojiya

Bring to a boil twice as much soup stock as rice, add the rice and slowly mix. Put the cover on and bring to a boil over high flame. After boiling, cook for 45-60 minutes over a low flame without stirring. When done, serve immediately. If you wait until the ojiya cools, it will be sticky like glue; so you should serve it while it is still hot.

Creating the Best Condiments for Ojiya

1. Chicken or fish goes best with kombu stock.
2. Vegetables or tofu goes best with kombu stock with bonita or chuba iriko (small dried fish).
3. Ojiya stock should taste a little saltier than clear broth.

How To Use Various Ingredients

Shellfish cooked for a long time get hard, so after ojiya comes to a boil, remove the shellfish to another bowl until the ojiya has cooked completely. Then return the shellfish to the pot.

If you have used fish and it gives the ojiya too fishy a taste, add parsley, watercress, or scallions; mix into pot just before turning off the flame. This gives more flavor and removes the fishy smell.

Condiments for Ojiya

Any of the following may be used: Grated fresh ginger, sarashi-negi (see pg. 80), roasted crushed nori, or minced orange rind.

Egg Ojiya

> 1 Tbsp oil
> 1 6" carrot
> 1 bu. scallions
> 6 cups soup stock*
> 1-4" daikon, cut tanzaku (see pg. 141)
> 3 cups cooked rice
> 2 tsp salt
> 2-4 eggs, fertile, organic

Heat oil, sauté scallions, then add daikon and carrot and sauté. Add the soup stock and bring to boil. Then add the salt and cooked rice; bring to boil over high flame Turn low and cook for thirty-five minutes. Beat eggs, then pour over the ojiya. Turn off flame. Mix and serve immediately.

If you like vegetable ojiya, then you may use kombu stock as mentioned below. However, any kind of soup is okay. You choose whichever you like. Also, you can season with miso instead of traditional soy sauce. All kinds of ojiya make you feel warm, so that they are good for winter or cold days.

* Kombu stock
> 3" x 12" piece of dashi kombu
> 7 cups water

Place kombu in pan. Add water and cook for one hour. Leave cover slightly ajar to prevent boiling over. Strain and use stock.

	Protein grams	Methionine/Cystine grams
1 bunch scallions	2.4	0.022
1-4" daikon	0.6	0.001
1 carrot	0.6	0.020
3 cups cooked rice	11.1	0.356
2-4 eggs	14.0	0.700
Total	28.7	1.099
MDR		100%

Albi Nishime (serves 5)

> 10 medium albi
> 1 tsp oil
> ½ tsp salt
> 2 tsp soy sauce

Scrub albi and scrape off outer hairy skin. Heat oil and sauté whole albi. Add ½ cup cold water, ¼ teaspoon salt and bring to a boil. Cook 20 minutes. Add ¼ teaspoon salt and soy sauce. Cook until tender.

It will be less salty when cold on the following day. Serve 2 albi per person.

	Protein grams	Methionine/Cystine grams
10 medium albi	8.6	0.095
2 tsp soy sauce	1.3	0.026
Total	9.9	0.121
MDR per serving		2.2%

Vegetable Hoto (serves 5)

> 3 cups whole wheat pastry flour or unbleached
> white flour

Add enough water to make the dough a little stiffer than ear-lobe consistency. Roll out to ⅛-inch thickness, cut into ⅓-inch strips.

> Five 1" square pieces of winter squash
> 1 bunch scallions, cut into 1" lengths, separate
> green and white parts
> 1 carrot, hangetsu (see pg. 140)
> ½ pkg. seitan, soaked and minced (6 oz)
> 3 tsp oil
> 1 tsp salt
> 2-3 Tbsp soy sauce
> 3½ cups soup stock,* mixed with same amount of
> water

* For soup stock, see recipe for kombu stock on page 97.

Put 1 teaspoon of oil in a heated pan, sauté the green part of the scallions. When the color changes, remove to another bowl. Add the remaining oil to the pan, sauté the white part of the scallions, add the squash, carrot, and seitan, in that order. Then add the diluted soup stock. When the vegetables begin to soften, slowly add the cut noodles and salt, mix from top to bottom to prevent sticking. Cook on a high flame until the soup boils, then turn down to a medium flame. Cook until the noodles are tender, add the soy sauce. Serve immediately in large bowls, placing the green part of the scallion in the soup bowl, over which the soup is poured. This soup warms the body quickly in winter. The taste improves with time, so it is very delicious when eaten as a leftover.

	Protein grams	Methionine/Cystine grams
3 cups w.w. pastry flour	36.0	1.554
1 bunch scallion	2.4	0.022
½ pkg. seitan (6/10 cup)	57.8	1.192
2-3 Tbsp soy sauce	3.8	0.080
MDR per serving		11.2%

Yose-Nabe (serves 5)

½ lb. chicken (or shrimp, shelled and de-veined)
10 oysters, washed in salted water
2 hard-boiled eggs, cut in quarters
5 medium shiitake mushrooms, soaked and cut
  ¼"-½" pieces
2 carrots, cut flower shape and precooked a few
  minutes
1 bu. watercress, top leaves only
1 scallion, cut on diagonal ¼" pieces
½ head Chinese cabbage, use inner leaves only
4 cups soup stock*
2 Tbsp soy sauce
2 tsp salt
½ lb whole wheat noodles or saifun, soaked overnight in boiling water

Cut Chinese cabbage koguchigiri-style in 2" pieces and place in the center of the pan. Place the chicken, shiitake, carrots, oysters, and watercress around the cabbage. Bring soup stock to a boil in another pot and add salt and soy sauce. After it has boiled, put it over the vegetables, bring to a boil again, and cook until the vegetables are tender. As you serve, add more items to the nabe pan.

* For the soup stock of this recipe, you can use kombu stock recipe which is the following:

Kombu stock
3" x 12" piece of dashi kombu
7 cups water

Place kombu in pan. Add water and cook for one hour. Leave cover slightly ajar to prevent boiling over. Strain and use stock.

	Protein grams	Methionine/Cystine grams
½ lb chicken	45.4	1.848
10 oysters	28.1	1.194
2 eggs	12.8	1.194*
2 Tbsp soy sauce	3.8	0.080
½ lb w.w. noodle	29.1	0.990
Total	119.2	4.812
MDR per serving		17.4%

* These values have been substituted by the values shrimp.

Buckwheat-Potato Casserole

> 1 cup cooked buckwheat groats
> 4-5 Idaho potatoes
> 1 chopped onion
> Chopped parsley
> **Mix together:**
> Dash of salt
> 2 beaten eggs
> Soy sauce
> 2 cups cooked rice-cream or kokoh
> ½ cup feta or goat-milk cheese

Slice the potatoes thin, place them into a greased baking dish, in alternate layers; potatoes, buckwheat, onions, parsley, and the liquid until all ingredients are used. Top with cheese if desired and bake approximately 1 hour at 350 degrees or until done.

	Protein grams	Methionine/Cystine grams
1 cup cooked buckwheat groats	5.9	0.217
4-5 potatoes	4.0	0.088
1 onion	0.7	0.006
1 parsley	2.5	0.012
2 eggs	12.8	0.700
2 cups cooked rice cream	7.5	0.237
½ cup goat milk cheese	12.5	0.368
Total	45.9	1.628
MDR		140%

Nikomi Oden (Vegetable Oden, serves 5)

8" piece daikon, cut in ¾" rounds
3" carrot, cut in ¼" wagiri (see pg. 139)
7 albi, washed well
1 large lotus root, cut in ⅓" rounds
½ piece konnyaku, cut in 6 pieces
¼ lb stringbeans, cut in 2" long pieces
kampyo (gourd strips)
5½ cups water
2 Tbsp soy sauce
8" piece dashi kombu
2 tsp salt
mustard (see recipe below)

Cook the lotus root in water to cover, in which two salt plums have been added, to keep it white in color. Cook just part way, not until tender. Cook daikon with 1 tablespoon sweet brown rice (in a cloth bag) in salted water until tender—about thirty five minutes. In a pot of salted water, cook the carrot and albi, also just part way.

In a big pot, bring the 5½ cups water to a boil and add the kombu, konnyaku, and the four cooked vegetables. Add more water to cover if necessary. Also put 1 teaspoon salt and 2 tablespoons soy sauce. Continue to cook for twenty minutes more. Add more soy sauce as desired. Tie the string beans with the kampyo and add them to the pot last. Serve this dish with mustard as a condiment.

To make the mustard: 2 tablespoons dry mustard and 1 tablespoon green or bancha hot tea mixed well in an oven-proof bowl. Invert the bowl over the burner on low heat for about 5-10 minutes until it gives off a potent mustard smell and is slightly browned. Serve on the table, to be mixed with soy sauce or oden sauce. This is a very good condiment for Chinese cabbage pickle or pressed salad. Do not eat if you have a pilonidal cyst (tail bone cyst).

	Protein grams	Methionine/Cystine grams
3" carrot	0.6	0.020
7 albi	8.6	0.095
1 large lotus root		
½ piece konnyaku		
¼ lb stringbeans	3.2	0.048
2 Tbsp soy sauce	3.8	0.080
Total	16.2	0.243
Serving one:	3.2	0.048
MDR per serving		1%

* These values are taken from *Food Values of Portions Commonly Used* by Bowes & Church without values on Cystine.

Chicken Stew Country Style (serves 5)

1-2 pieces chicken meat
¼ onion, cut ¼" thickness
½ medium daikon, cut ichogaki (see pg. 140),
    ¼" thick half moons
1 medium carrot, cut as daikon
1 konnyaku, cut by scraping with a wine cup
1 medium burdock, cut sasagaki (see pg. 141)
1 lb albi, cut ½" rangiri (see pg. 139)
⅓ cup green peas (fresh or dried)
1 Tbsp oil
5 cups soup stock*
1½ tsp salt
1½ Tbsp soy sauce
2 Tbsp kuzu
3 medium shiitake. Soak and remove stems.

Heat oil, sauté the burdock, shiitake, daikon, carrot, and konnyaku. When color changes, add the chicken, albi, and green peas. Sauté a short time and add a pinch of salt. Add the soup stock or boiling water and bring to a boil. Add salt and soy sauce and cook on medium heat. (Note: Taste the vegetables, not just the soup stock, before salting.) Dissolve kuzu and add to soup. Serve hot with a side dish of rice or bread.

In hunting season, there may be quail, pheasant, or other hunter's luck available.

* For the soup stock of this recipe, you may use kombu soup stock, which is as follows:

Kombu stock
3" x 12" piece of dashi kombu
7 cups water

Place kombu in pan. Add water and cook for one hour. Leave cover slightly ajar to prevent boiling over. Strain and use stock.

	Protein grams	Methionine/Cystine grams
1-2 pieces chicken meat	10.2	0.407
1 carrot	0.6	0.020
1 lb albi	8.6	0.095
⅓ cup green peas	3.4	0.063
1½ Tbsp soy sauce	2.9	0.060
3 shiitake mushrooms	0.8	0.020
Total	26.5	0.665
Serving one:	5.3	0.133
MDR per serving		2.4%

Tazukuri (Dry Fish) A (serves 5)

> 1 cup tazukuri
> 1 Tbsp oil
> 3 Tbsp soy sauce

Heat oil. Sauté fish until crispy. Add soy sauce and keep shaking pan to distribute sauce evenly. Cook until dry. Do not use chopsticks to stir fish as they break heads and tails off.

	Protein grams	Methionine/Cystine grams
1 cup tazukuri	81.8	3.481*
3 Tbsp soy sauce	5.7	0.120
Total	87.5	3.765
Serving one:	17.5	0.753
MDR per serving		13.6%

*This value is based on the value of cod

Tazukuri B (serves 10)

> 2 cups tazukuri
> 2 Tbsp Japanese sake (rice wine)
> 2 Tbsp soy sauce
> 1 Tbsp Yinnie syrup

Roast tazukuri in dry skillet until well-dried and brownish in color. In another pan cook together, uncovered over low flame, soy sauce, Yinnie syrup, and sake for 5 minutes until mixture becomes thick. Add roasted fish and shake pan until sauce covers fish.

Remove to a dish to cool. Yinnie is good with this crispy fish dish.

This recipe is almost double the MDR value of A.

Lentil Soup (serves 6)

> 1 cup lentils soaked in 2 cups water and cooked by
>   pressure for 20 minutes
> 3 med. onions, cut thin mawashigiri (see pg. 141)
> 1 carrot, cut ichogiri (¼" moon shape, see pg. 140)
> ½ stalk celery, cut ¼" sainome (see pg. 140)
> 1 Tbsp oil
> 4-5 cups water
> 2 tsp salt
> 1 tsp soy sauce

Heat oil, sauté onion until brown, add carrot, sauté few minutes, add celery, sauté few minutes, add to boiling water, and cook for 20 minutes over medium flame. Add cooked lentils and salt, and cook for 30 minutes.

Season well with soy sauce and serve hot. Sprinkle with minced parsley.

	Protein grams	Methionine/Cystine grams
1 cup lentils	50.0	1.536
3 onions	2.1	0.018
1 carrot	0.6	0.020
½ stalk celery	0.3	0.005
1 tsp soy sauce	0.4	0.012
Total	53.4	1.591
Serving one:	8.9	0.265
MDR per serving		4%

CHAPTER 4

Other Soybean and Higher Protein Foods

1. Tofu

Tofu, a food made from soybeans, is not well known in this country. In the Orient, on the other hand, tofu has been one of the important foods for centuries. It has a bland taste so that it can be flavored with seasonings or with other food materials to give a variety of tasty products.

To make tofu requires three steps: preparation of soybean milk, coagulation of protein, and formation of tofu cubes in a mold.

(a) Preparation of Soybean Milk

One pound of soybeans are washed and soaked in water at room temperature for four to five hours or until the beans swell. Then the swollen soybeans are blended until finely ground.

(b) Coagulation of Soybean Protein

To the soybean milk from the preceding step is added eight times as much water. This is heated to boiling and reduced to about one-third. Cool the milk to about 80° C. (176° F.), add about 1 tablespoon of nigari ($MgCl$) to the milk very slowly, and gently mix with a scoop to prevent a breakdown of the curd that forms. Then put the curd in a cloth and squeeze out the excess water.

The coagulation of soybean protein by the addition of nigari is the most difficult step in making tofu. The right amount of nigari and the proper rate of its addition are two important factors necessary to attain a satisfactory curd. The addition of insufficient amounts of nigari or the addition of nigari too fast causes incomplete coagulation. If too much nigari is added, the tofu will be too hard.

Generally, market tofu is coagulated by adding calcium sulfate ($CaSO_2$) or magnesium sulfate ($MgSO_2$). $CaSO_2$ causes a slower, smoother, and softer coagulation than $MgSO_2$ does. For natural macrobiotic tofu, we use nigari instead of these chemicals. To make nigari ($MgCl$), wet crude salt a little and put in a coarse bag such as a gunny sack or hemp bag. Keep this in a dark and humid place so that the salt gradually absorbs water from the air. $MgCl$ precipitates from the bag. The accumulation of this liquid is nigari.

(c) The Formation of Tofu in a Mold

The curd looks like cottage cheese. After it has settled and when its temperature has dropped to about 122° F, it is gently transferred with a ladle to a wooden box, lined with a double-layered cheesecloth.

The box (about 6" long x 4" wide x 6" deep) has small holes in its sides and bottom to drain off the water. The curd is pressed by a light handpress weighing about one pound. When the weight stops, the product is cakelike and ready to be removed from the box.

For recipes, please read the *Do of Cooking*.

(d) Tofu for External Treatment

Tofu is not only a very delicious food but also very important as a medicine if you know how to use it. Always keep one or two tofu pieces in your refrigerator so that you can use it to make tofu, which has miraculous curing power in the following cases:

Apply tofu plaster to the head in case of internal hemorrhage. It is also good for a high temperature, headache, and fever.

To make tofu plaster, squeeze out water from tofu, add 10 percent wheat flour, and knead. Add more flour if dough is too watery. Change plaster every two hours. However, for critical cases, change it every twenty minutes. Do not use plastic or rubber materials to spread the plaster on because they do not "breathe." Use cotton flannel.

Note: tofu plaster is applied only to the head or neck.

(e) Agé—Deep Fried Tofu

Slice tofu about 1" x 2" x ⅓" thick and drain off water. Then deep fry in vegetable oil. This is very good for miso soup. Miso soup is sometimes difficult to make attractive for children. This can be accomplished by adding agé, which will give miso soup a milder taste.

2. Natto

Natto is a fermented soybean product and is not well known to most Americans, though it has been used by many Japanese families for centuries. It has an unusual taste that is not easy for some modern people to appreciate. But just as enemies can become your best friends, natto can grow on you if you are persistent. It has a faint resemblance to Roquefort cheese, perhaps, because both are high in protein and both are the result of fermentation. It serves as an excellent source of protein for non-meat-eating people. It is available in Japanese markets if you cannot find the time to make your own.

Soybeans are difficult to digest. However, by allowing bacteria to digest them for us, which occurs in the process of making miso, soy sauce, and natto, they become a very nutritious, easily assimilable food. Natto is the simplest soybean preparation. It is more yang than tofu but more yin than miso or soy sauce because it has neither the yang factor of time nor salt applied.

It will keep for months in the refrigerator, and can be served at any time with no preparation; thus, it is good to have around for unexpected attacks of hunger or hungry guests.

To make natto, soak matured dry soybeans overnight in water and boil until tender. Drain off the water and allow to partially air-dry in a bamboo tray for twenty minutes. Then put rice straw on the bottom of metal pans. The beans are then placed in the pans and covered with rice straw, then placed in ovens at approximately 95° F. for one day.

The finished product has a dark tan color, and the beans retain their shape but are covered by a stringy, slimy substance.

To serve natto, mix with traditional soy sauce and stir well. Radish leaves or chopped scallion add zest, color, and flavor. It is best eaten with rice.

3. How to Make Natto at Home

> 3 cups soybeans
> 5 cups water
> 5, 1 pint paper containers

Wash soybeans, soak in 5 cups water overnight (do not pressure cook). In a regular pot, bring to a boil over a high flame, lower the flame, and cook for 4-5 hours until the beans are tender; do not stir or the beans will break. Water will almost all boil off; a little bit should be left. Place one (1) heaping cup of hot soybeans in a cardboard container, fold in the top cover. Put all the filled containers in a double paper bag. Close up the bag, tie it with string, and put the bag in the oven. The oven should be 140° or the heat of the pilot light only; do not turn the oven any higher. Leave the soybeans in the oven for three nights. Take out after the third night, as they should be ready. If you cook a larger quantity of beans, it is necessary to stack the containers one on top of the other. After the second night, switch the top to the bottom and vice-versa. Let them stay another full day. Do not use your oven while you are making natto. These fermented soybeans (natto) are very good for digestion and a good source of protein.

This natto can be kept frozen about one-two months and refrigerated about a week. To serve this, make the following "Scrambled Natto":

Scrambled Natto

> 1 container natto
> ⅛ tsp salt
> 1 Tbsp soy sauce
> 2 heaping Tbsp sliced scallion or daikon leaves

Mix Natto, salt, and soy sauce. Then scramble the mixture well. Add chopped scallion or daikon leaves and scramble again. Serve with rice. To eat, put 1 teaspoon full of Scrambled Natto on the rice and eat together.

Scrambled Natto is a good source of protein. You can stop a craving for animal foods by eating Scrambled Natto.

Protein and Essential Amino Acid Contents of Natto and their percentages to the Minimum Daily Requirement

	grams	MDR%
Protein	16.5	
Tryptophan	0.280	112
Threonine	0.750	150
Isoleucine	0.870	124
Leucine	1.360	123
Lysine	0.950	118
Methionine	0.180	90
Methionine/Cystine	0.430	39
Phenylalanine	0.900	300
Phenylalanine/Tyrosine	1.510	137
Valine	0.980	122

Based on "Scientific Research Council of Japan."

Tofu, Seitan, and Gluten Cooking for Warmer Times

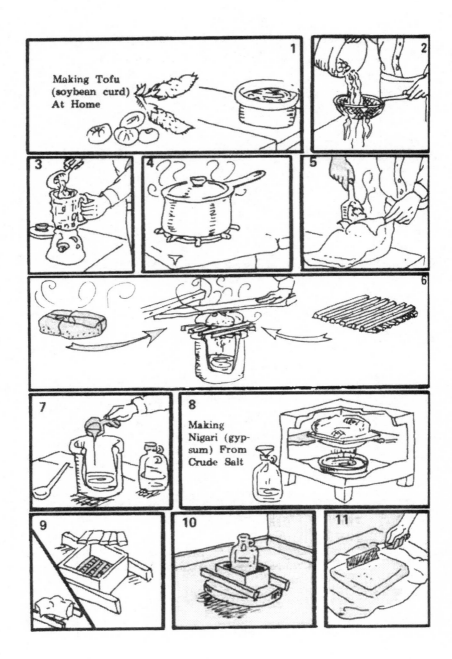

Tofu Making

3 cups green soybeans
6 cups water
3 Tbsp nigari*

Soak soybeans overnight in water (figure 1). In summer, seven hours is sufficient; in winter, if it is very cold, soak beans for twenty hours. To test, cut a bean in half; inside and outside should be the same color. Drain beans, reserving water (figure 2).

Blend beans in an electric blender or force through a food mill (figure 3), adding some of the soaking water, if necessary, to make a paste. Bring twenty-five cups of water to a boil (figure 4), and add purged beans immediately to avoid spoiling. Bring beans to a boil without cover and stir. Sprinkle cold water on beans to quiet bubbling. Repeat three times, always bringing the water back to a boil.

Place several cotton flour sacks in a wooden keg and pour bean mixture into a sack (figure 5), then place in keg to reserve liquid. Squeeze sack to remove water (figure 6). Sprinkle nigari over the water drained from the beans (figure 7). Note: Bean water must be hot in order for nigari to work. Let it rest five minutes. With a long-handled wooden spoon, make two deep strokes into the water at right angles to each other (as though to form a cross). Make these strokes slowly as though you were going to lift the bottom matter up to the top of the keg—dipping in at the side of the keg and coming up again in the center.

Let rest again for ten minutes, checking to see if liquid separated. If not, sprinkle another tablespoon of nigari over water. Let it stand five minutes and repeat two deep strokes with wooden spoon. Wait five minutes again. You will see a white thickened substance resembling scrambled eggs.

Line a square box with a slatted bottom (figure 9) with a clean cotton cloth and spoon out the thick white substance into the towel. Cover the top of the container with a cloth and then a wooden lid. Place an empty quart jar on the lid for pressure (figure 10). One hour later increase pressure by using a ½ gallon jug containing four cups water. About 1½ hours later all water should be drained and tofu is ready to use. Place container in sink and slowly remove cover and towels. Cover tofu with cold water for thirty minutes before serving. Cut into pieces 3" x 4½" and one inch thick (figure 11). Makes 6 blocks of tofu.

More notes on tofu: Water should be squeezed from tofu slowly, otherwise it becomes hard and breaks easily. The water is light brown in color. Spring water is best to use when making tofu.

Tofu will keep one week, covered in water and refrigerated. Change the water every two days to keep tofu fresh.

* Nigari: To make nigari, use damp sea salt. If the sea salt is dry, sprinkle it with some water until fairly damp. Place salt in cloth and gather sides to make a sack. Hang sack in a cool, damp place to drain for several days. Collect the liquid that drips from the cloth sack into a pan or bucket—this liquid is nigari. (See figure 8 on page 112.)

Quantity: Tofu Preparation

> 10 lbs soybeans
> 18 gallons water
> 1½-2 cups nigari

Proceed as for regular tofu.

Ten pounds soybeans will make nine pounds of tofu that will be 24 pieces 4" x 4" x 4". Therefore, one piece of tofu contains:

	Protein grams	Methionine/Cystine grams
9 lbs tofu	243.0	6.075
1 piece tofu (4" x 4" x 4")	10.0	0.253
MDR		23%

Okara or Unohana (serves 5)

> 3 cups okara (the remains from tofu making)
> 1 cup burdock, sasagaki (see pg. 141)
> 1 cup carrot, sasagaki
> 1 cup onion, mawashigiri (see pg. 141)
> ½ cup green onions, cut in ¼" pieces
> ½ Tbsp soy sauce
> 2 Tbsp oil
> 1 tsp salt

Sauté burdock in oil until the smell is gone; add onion. When the onions become transparent, add carrots. Sauté a few minutes and add salt and soy sauce. Cook with cover over medium flame for thirty minutes. When all vegetables are tender, add scallions and soybean purée. If too dry, add ¼ cup water. Cook with a cover over medium flame for fifteen minutes, then mix from bottom to top. Cover and cook five more minutes. Then mix again until beans are hot.

Serve as a side dish with rice, or mix into the rice. Or put pressure-cooked rice into a casserole in a layer about 1" thick. Cut into squares and serve.

Variation: Okara can be used in croquettes with pastry flour and minced vegetables. Okara is also good in clear soup. Yin, sick people should not eat okara dishes.

	Protein grams	Methionine/Cystine grams
3 cups okara (300 gms.)	10.5	0.240
1 cup carrot	0.6	0.005
1 cup onion	2.0	0.020
½ cup scallions	0.6	0.008
½ Tbsp soy sauce	0.6	0.020
Total	14.3	0.293
MDR per serving		1.6%

Hiya Tofu

Hiya yako (cold, uncooked tofu) tastes very good in summer. Slice tofu and serve on a glass plate. Tofu is quite watery, so tilt plate to one side and drain off excess liquid. Serve with ginger soy sauce sauce (five tablespoons soy sauce, one teaspoon grated fresh ginger, and mix together) or lemon juice sauce (one tablespoon soy sauce and one tablespoon lemon juice). Use whichever you like. Tofu spoils very quickly, so cover with cold water and keep in the refrigerator. Change water every two days. It can keep for about one week. If tofu floats on the surface, this means it is spoiling. Do not use it.

Kanten Tofu (Tofu Aspic)

1½ blocks of fresh tofu
1 tsp green lemon or lime peel
1 kanten bar
2 cups water

Slice tofu into six pieces and add it to eight cups of boiling water. Then bring to a boil again. Pour off liquid and save. Mash tofu in suribachi. Soak kanten in two cups of water for 20 minutes, breaking it into small pieces. Bring to a boil and cook for twenty minutes. Remove pan from the heat, and set aside to cool without cover. After becoming lukewarm, add it to the tofu in the suribachi and grind well. Repeat a few times adding liquid and grinding until all the liquid is used. Then pour it into a mold and put in the refrigerator. After it hardens, take it out of the mold and cut it into 4" long, match-thin strips. Then place on a glass plate and decorate with boiled string beans cut thin. Serve with sarashi-negi (see pg. 80) condiment and sauce as follows:

½ cup soup stock*
2 tablespoons soy sauce
¼ cup freshly shaved bonita

Mix sauce and water and bring to a boil. Add bonita and bring to a boil uncovered. Remove from the pan, and set aside to cool. Then strain through a cotton cloth. Don't waste the bonita. You can use it in a clear soup or miso soup or nitsuké.

* Soup Stock
3" x 12" piece of dashi kombu
7 cups water

Place kombu in pan. Add water and cook 1 hour. Leave cover slightly ajar to prevent boiling over. Strain and use stock.
  Try this sauce for variety:

Vinegar Sauce
5 Tbsp rice vinegar
2 Tbsp soy sauce
1 Tbsp Mirin

Mix well. Or, if you don't have string beans, grate green lemon or lime peel and sprinkle it on top of the tofu.

	Protein grams	Methionine/Cystine grams
1½ blocks of tofu (300 gm.)	18.0	0.450
1 kanten bar	1.4	0.060
Total	19.4	0.510
MDR		46%

Nori-Maki (Tofu Rolled in Nori)

> 2 pieces tofu
> ½ tsp salt
> ½ cup soaked & chopped mushrooms
> 1½ Tbsp soy sauce
> ⅓ cup string beans, thinly sliced
> 3 sheets nori seaweed
> 1 Tbsp sesame oil
> 6 kampyo (gourd strips)

Mash the tofu in a suribachi and set aside. Heat oil and sauté first the mushrooms (shiitake is best to use), string beans, and finally the carrots. Add a small amount of water left over from soaking mushrooms and salt and cover pan. Cook fifteen minutes. Remove cover, add soy sauce, and continue cooking for another five minutes over a high flame to remove excess liquid.

Lightly toast nori and place on a sushi (bamboo) mat. Mix tofu thoroughly with vegetables. Spread a layer of tofu mixture ½ inch thick over nori sheets, leaving a one-inch border on the two lengthwise sides of the nori.

Using the sushi mat, roll the nori lengthwise. Wash gourd strips in warm water to soften them, and tie at each end of the nori rolls.

Place rolls in a vegetable or cous-cous steamer and steam for ten minutes. Let cool. Slice into one-inch pieces and serve.

	Protein grams	Methionine/Cystine grams
2 pieces tofu (400 gm.)	24.0	0.600
½ cup mushrooms	4.0	0.083
⅓ cup string beans	0.8	0.012
1½ Tbsp soy sauce	2.9.	0.060
3 sheets nori	8.5	0.400
Total	40.2	1.155
MDR		100%

Tofu Kuzu Aspic

1½ blocks tofu (squeeze out water by twisting it in
    a cotton cloth)
½ medium carrot, cut in small 1" long sengiri (see
    pg. 140)
2 medium scallions, cut ⅛" thick koguchigiri (see
    pg. 139)
1 agé (2" x ½" x ½") (fried tofu) cut lengthwise in
    sengiri
1 Tbsp kiku ragé (dried mushrooms), soaked in
    water and cut sengiri
¼ cup kuzu, dissolved in 1 cup cold water
3 Tbsp soy sauce
2 Tbsp sesame oil

Heat cooking pan, heat oil, and sauté scallions a little. Then add carrot, agé, and kiku ragé. Mash tofu in a cotton cloth, then sauté like scrambled eggs. Season with soy sauce. Add kuzu, then bring to a boil. Pour to cool in attractive flower-shaped bowl, custard bowl, or small leaf-shaped bowl, jello ring, etc., and set in the refrigerator to chill. Take out of mold and sprinkle with parsley.

	Protein grams	Methionine/Cystine grams
1½ block tofu	18.0	0.450
½ medium carrot	0.6	0.005
2 medium scallions	0.6	0.006
1 agé	0.4	0.011
1 Tbsp kiku ragé	0.8	0.017
¼ cup kuzu		
3 Tbsp soy sauce	5.7	0.120
Total	26.1	0.609
MDR		55%

Unagi Tofu (Mock Eel)

> 1 piece tofu
> small knob of fresh ginger root
> ½ tsp salt
> 1 Tbsp soy sauce
> ½ cup whole wheat pastry flour
> 1 sheet nori seaweed

Slice tofu into 6 pieces and add it to 8 cups of boiling water. Then bring to a boil again. Pour off liquid and save. Mash tofu in suribachi. If you don't have the time to prepare it like this, then place tofu in a clean cloth and squeeze over a sink to remove excess liquid. Add flour and salt to mashed tofu and mix well. Cut nori into four pieces and place on a flat surface. Cover each piece of nori with a ⅓ inch thick layer of tofu mixture. Heat oil to 350° F. Deep fry tofu pieces for only a few minutes with the nori side down. Remove when tofu is still light color. Do not brown. To prepare ginger, peel if the outside skin is hard, then grate with a fine grater. Squeeze out ginger juice. Mix 1 teaspoon ginger juice with soy sauce. When tofu is done, drain. Then pierce each piece with two skewers and brush with ginger soy sauce. Serve immediately.

	Protein grams	Methionine/Cystine grams
1 piece tofu	12.0	0.300
½ cup w.w. pastry flour	5.8	0.190
1 Tbsp soy sauce	1.9	0.040
1 sheet nori	3.0	0.130
Total	22.7	0.660
MDR		60%

Kaminari Tofu (Thunder Tofu)

5 medium shiitake mushrooms
1 cup water
½ tsp salt
⅓ cup fresh green peas
1 Tbsp soy sauce
1 carrot, minced
¼ cup chopped parsley
1 tsp sesame oil
6 cups cold water
2 pieces tofu, cut in half

Soak mushrooms in 1 cup water for twenty minutes. Remove and reserve water; chop mushrooms fine, discarding hard stems. Heat oil in pan and sauté mushrooms, then peas and carrots. Add ⅓ cup reserved mushroom water and salt.

Cover pan and cook twenty minutes. Add 1 tablespoon soy sauce half way through cooking. In a separate pot, bring 6 cups water to boil. Add tofu, strain immediately. Purée tofu. Add purée to the cooked vegetables and stir with chop sticks until it resembles scrambled eggs. If desired, season with soy sauce to taste.

Add parsley and stir until parsley is bright green.

Note: Any combination of vegetables and mushrooms can be used in this preparation. The name "Thunder Tofu" comes from the sound made during cooking.

	Protein grams	Methionine/Cystine grams
5 medium shiitake	8.0	0.167
⅓ cup green peas	4.3	0.030
1 carrot	0.6	0.005
2 pieces tofu	24.0	0.600
¼ cup parsley	0.6	0.003
Total	37.5	0.805
MDR		73%

Agé-Tofu (Stuffed Tofu): Variation

> 7 pieces agé (available in Asian markets)
> soy sauce
> vegetable mixture, prepared as above for Kaminari
>   Tofu
> kampyo (dried gourd strip)
> 2 Tbsp kuzu
> 3 Tbsp cold water
> 4 cups liquid (half soup stock, half water)

Cut agé in half. Open gently to make a pouch and stuff with vegetable mixture. Holding the stuffed agé, tie each bundle with gourd strips that have been washed in warm water. Punch about five or six holes in the sides of the agé with a toothpick and place in a pan. Cover with soup stock and water.

Bring to a boil and simmer for ten minutes. Add soy sauce and continue cooking for ten minutes.

Turn agé over gently and cook another ten minutes. Remove agé pouches. Add kuzu dissolved in cold water and bring to a boil. Remove from heat. Serve one tablespoon of sauce over each agé.

*Agé (pronounced ah-gae) is deep fried tofu.

	Protein grams	Methionine/Cystine grams
7 pieces agé	6.0	0.15
MDR		13%

Wheat Gluten

Wheat gluten is a valuable source of protein that has been used by people of many countries throughout history. It was first introduced to Japanese monks over 800 years ago when wheat was first brought over from China. Dry gluten, "fu," was known for many years before that time. Gluten was commonly prepared in the temples of Japan.

> 10 cups whole wheat flour
> 5 cups cold water
> 4 cups unbleached flour
> 2 tsp salt

Mix flours and add water in which the salt has been dissolved. Knead in a bowl. Continue kneading strongly until dough softens. (Note: this is best done by placing bowl on floor and kneading vigorously in a kneeling position.) The dough will not make good gluten unless it is well kneaded. Knead for twenty minutes or longer.

Set dough in a dry bowl and leave uncovered for forty minutes. Then add 8-10 cups cold water, knead vigorously, wring out all the cream-colored starch from dough. Change water, repeating this process 5-6 times, reserving the starch water to use in baking. Each time water is changed it will become less sedimented. When only slightly sedimented starch water is obtained, stop. Knead dough until it becomes rubbery. Place in a strainer. About five cups of gluten dough is obtained.

In a separate pot, bring 10-12 cups of water to a boil. Pull the gluten into thin one-inch pieces with your fingers, and drop into boiling water. Continue boiling until gluten rises to the top. (Note: when using ten cups of water, remove gluten pieces from boiling water and repeat, cooking one more time). Strain and reserve water to use in cooking. Wash the gluten in cold water one or two times until the gluten is completely cold. Gluten pieces must be completely cold before they are added to the soy sauce mixture when making seitan.

Gluten is easy to digest, a good source of protein for sick people. It is eaten in all seasons, especially by vegetarian and non-meat-eating people. Not only is it very important as a source of protein, but it is also very enjoyable. It is used in soups, stews, fried foods, etc. Seitan is made from wheat gluten.

	Protein grams	Methionine/Cystine grams
100 gm. gluten*	41.4	1.612
1 cup gluten	58.0	2.257
MDR		205%

* Taken from *Amino Acid Content of Foods, Home Economic Research Report No.4* published by U.S. Dept. of Agriculture.

Seitan

        1 Tbsp dark sesame oil
        1-2 cups soy sauce
        1 Tbsp minced ginger root
        5 cups cold cooked gluten

Heat oil in a sauce pan, add minced ginger (use only fresh ginger), and sauté. The amount of soy sauce used depends upon how long you intend to store the seitan. Use a larger amount of soy sauce for longer storing and refrigerating.

Add soy sauce, bring to a boil, and drop in pieces of gluten. Cook on low heat for three hours, stirring frequently. Remove cover and continue cooking until excess liquid is absorbed and evaporated.

Seitan is ideal as a seasoning in noodles au gratin, stews, cooked with vegetables, etc. It will keep for long periods of time in the refrigerator.

	Protein grams	Methionine/Cystine grams
1 cup soy sauce	18.7	0.640
5 cups gluten	560.0	11.285
Total	578.7	11.925
1 cup seitan	96.4	1.987
MDR		180%
2 Tbsp	12.05	0.248
1 Tbsp	6.02	0.124

Fresh Wheat Fu

> 6 cups wheat gluten, separated into two parts
> 8 cups water
> 3 cups each: sweet brown rice flour, whole wheat
>   pastry flour

Knead one part of the wheat gluten with three cups flour. As the gluten is very sticky, kneading will be difficult at first, but after about twenty minutes of kneading, the dough will become smooth. Repeat as above for the remaining gluten and flour.

Pat out each section into a rectangle about 5 x 6 inches and 2 inches thick. Bring water to a boil and drop in one rectangle. Once the water comes to a boil again, lower flame and let simmer for twenty minutes. If using a steamer, cook gluten over a high flame for thirty minutes

Remove gluten with a ladle and place on a platter to cool. Cut into strips ½-inch wide. Reserve water to use in cooking or baking. Water and cooked fu can be stored in a refrigerator for one week. Fu can be used in a variety of vegetable dishes or deep fried and served with noodles or stew.

	Protein grams	Methionine/Cystine grams
5 cups gluten	560.0	11.285
3 cups sweet rice flour	45.0	1.410
3 cups w.w. flour	40.0	1.770
Total	645.0	27.435

This recipe makes about 20 strips of Wheat Fu. Each Wheat Fu, therefore, contains:

	32.2	1.317
MDR		125%

Fried Fu—Gluten Cutlet (serves 10)

> 1 cup whole wheat pastry flour
> tempura oil
> 5 strips cooked fu (made from either sweet brown
>   rice or whole wheat pastry flour)
> 2 cups tempura batter
> 2 cups corn meal, bread crumbs, or cracked wheat

Dust fu strips with pastry flour, then dip into tempura batter, cover with corn meal, and let sit on a plate for about five minutes.

Deep fry in hot oil (350 degrees) turning over once after strips rise to the top of oil. Cutlets take about five minutes to cook. Remove from oil with a strainer or slotted spoon and place in a strainer set inside another pan to catch excess oil before serving.

Serving suggestions: cut carrots and cabbage leaves into thin strips and sauté in a small amount of oil with a pinch of salt over a high flame for about five minutes.

Make a bed of the sautéed vegetables in the center of a serving dish and place cutlets on top. Garnish with red radishes cut into flower shapes.

	Protein grams	Methionine/Cystine grams
1 cup w.w. pastry flour	16.0	0.590
5 strips Fu	161.5	6.860
2 cups tempura batter	23.0	0.760
2 cups corn meal*	22.0	0.680
Total	222.5	8.890
MDR per serving		80%

* taken from *Nutrition Almanac* by John O. Kirschmann, published by Nutrition Search, 1973

Tofu, Seitan, and Gluten
Cooking for Colder Times

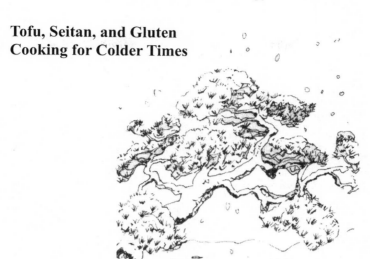

Shinano-agé (Fried Tofu with Buckwheat)

2 pieces of tofu (2" x ½" x ½")
½ cup buckwheat flour
tempura oil
cotton cloth

Sauce
½ cup soup stock
½ cup cold water
3 Tbsp soy sauce
4-5 scallions

Prepare scallions first by washing in cold water, then cutting as thinly as possible in sarashi-negi style (see pg.80). Use only two inches of the green sections, reserving the tops for use in other dishes.

Dip pieces of tofu into buckwheat flour and then deep fry in hot (350 degree) oil until golden, or pan fry. If pan frying, cover the pan while cooking the first side of the tofu then remove cover, turn tofu over, and fry other side.

While the tofu is cooking, bring soup stock water and soy sauce to a boil and simmer for just one minute. Remove from heat.

Serve sarashi-negi scallions as a garnish with the tofu and soup stock sauce.

	Protein grams	Methionine/Cystine grams
2 pieces of tofu	0.8	0.011
½ cup buckwheat flour	5.7	0.210
3 Tbsp soy sauce	3.6	0.120
4-5 scallions	1.2	0.012
Total	11.3	0.353
MDR		32%

Vegetable Tofu Stew with Lemon Sauce

> 5 scallions, cut into 1½" diagonal
> 2 pieces tofu, cut in 1" squares
> ½ head Chinese cabbage, boil a few minutes
> ½ bunch spinach (roll cabbage with spinach inside
>   and cut into 1" slices)
> 1 carrot, cut flower shape in ⅛" thickness
> 1 burdock, cut on long diagonal ⅛" thick
> 4" piece dashi kombu
> 12" piece Nagaimo*, cut ¼" thick on diagonal
> 4 cups water, about 1" from top of pot
> salt

Place kombu on the bottom of the pot. Add vegetables and water and cook until vegetables are done. Add salt and soy sauce and serve. Keep a small pitcher of extra soup stock and soy sauce on the table to be added according to individual desires. (For lemon juice sauce, see Hiya Tofu on page 116).

* Nagaimo is a long hairy root vegetable available in Japanese markets. It is light tan on the outside and white inside.

	Protein grams	Methionine/Cystine grams
5 scallions	2.4	0.022
2 tofu pieces	24.0	0.600
½ Chinese cabbage	2.6	0.024
½ bunch spinach	2.3	0.085
1 carrot	0.6	0.020
Total	31.9	0.751
MDR		68%

Oyster Nabe (serves 6)

> 1 lb fresh oysters, washed in salt water and drained
> 2 bunches of scallions, cut hasugiri (see pg. 140)
> 2 bunches of watercress
> 1 block tofu, cut into ten 1-inch squares
> ½ pkg. harusame (bean starch noodles) available at
>   Japanese markets, cooked in water five minutes
> 2 cups soup stock, see pg. 117
> ½ tsp salt
> 2 Tbsp soy sauce

Decorate a big plate with all ingredients. Bring to a boil soup stock, add salt and soy sauce and ½ the remaining ingredients. Bring to a boil and serve steaming hot at the table. Keep it hot at the table on a hot plate or heating unit. After serving the first time, add the rest of the ingredients.

A sprinkle of orange rind on each dish is nice when you serve.

	Protein grams	Methionine/Cystine grams
1 lb oyster	84.9	3.614
2 bunches scallions	4.8	0.044
2 bunches watercress	4.4	0.026
1 block tofu	12.0	0.300
½ pkg. harusame		
2 Tbsp soy sauce	3.8	0.080
Total	109.9	4.064
MDR per serving		10%

Chiri-Nabe (serves 5)

> 1 lb white meat such as cod, red snapper, or bass (if
> you use whole fish, cut the head into 1½" square
> pieces, rub with 1 Tbsp salt to remove the strong
> smell, wash off completely before using)
> 1 piece tofu
> 5 scallions, cut on ¼" long diagonals
> 2 turnips, cut mawashigiri (see pg. 141)
> 2 bunches watercress or spinach
> 5 cups water
> 6" piece kombu
> 3 Tbsp sake
> Optional: Sardines, celery, fresh mushrooms, Chi-
> nese cabbage

Soak kombu in water for two hours with sake. Bring to a boil and remove kombu. Add fish and turnips, cook until they are tender. Then
add scallions and watercress. Cook only for a few minutes. Add tofu.
Serve with lemon sauce in a side dish. This dish is not oily, rich, or
heavy; it has a very delicate enjoyable taste. If you have leftover
soup stock or sauce, it can be served over noodles.

To make lemon sauce:
> 1 Tbsp lemon juice
> 1 Tbsp soy sauce
> ¼ tsp grated ginger (optional)
> 1 scallion, minced and washed (optional)

Mix ingredients in a dish and serve on the side.

	Protein grams	Methionine/Cystine grams
1 lb cod	74.9	3.187
1 tofu piece	12.0	0.182
5 scallions	2.4	0.022
2 turnips	1.4	0.045
2 bunches watercress	4.4	0.026
Total	95.1	3.462
MDR per serving		12.4%

Celery-Sesame Salad (serves 5)

> 3 stalks celery
> 1-2 Tbsp soy sauce
> 5 Tbsp black sesame seeds

Slice celery very thin diagonally and place in strainer. Dip strainer in and out of pan of boiling water. Shake strainer to cool celery.

Roast sesame seeds until easily crushed between thumb and fourth finger. Grind seeds in suribachi into butter. Add soy sauce and mix until creamy.

Add cooled celery to creamy sauce after squeezing out excess water in celery between the palms. Mix thoroughly in sauce and serve or place celery in small individual plates and top with sesame sauce.

	Protein grams	Methionine/Cystine grams
3 stalks celery	2.0	0.031
5 Tbsp sesame seeds	13.7	0.804
1 Tbsp soy sauce	1.9	0.040
Total	17.6	0.875
MDR per serving		3%

Sesame Sauce

> 5 tsp roasted ground sesame seeds
> 8 tsp soy sauce

Grind well and mix together. If you want a thicker sauce, bring to a boil and evaporate. Good for cooked vegetable salad, baked or boiled fish. A flavorful, highly nutritious sauce.

	Protein grams	Methionine/Cystine grams
5 tsp sesame seeds	9.1	0.300
8 tsp soy sauce	3.0	0.102
Total	12.0	0.402
MDR		38%

Shish Kebabs (serves 6)

> 4 carrots or 3 burdock roots
> ½ tsp salt
> water
> 3 strips cooked fu
> tempura oil
> 12-15 wooden skewers

Cut each piece of fu into six pieces. Cut vegetables into logs 1½ inches long. Boil carrots in just enough water to cover with salt for fifteen minutes. Carrots should be tender, but still firm. If using burdock, use only the upper portion to maintain a diameter of about ¾ inch. Burdock may be pressure-cooked for fifteen minutes with ½ teaspoon salt and ¼ inch of water in pressure cooker. If boiling, cook burdock for about forty-five minutes in salted water.

Using the same amount of flour and tempura batter as for the gluten cutlet (see pg. 126), dip vegetables first into flour, then batter, and finally into corn meal or bread crumbs. Deep fry in oil. Repeat for the pieces of wheat fu.

Drain as for gluten cutlets, then alternate pieces of fu with vegetables on wooden skewers.

Serving suggestion: In the center of a platter, make a bed of string beans or snow peas that have been cooked in salted water. Surround with a layer of salad greens and arrange shish kebabs on top of leaves.

	Protein grams	Methionine/Cystine grams
4 carrots	5.6	0.240
3 strips cooked fu	96.6	4.116
Total	102.2	4.356
MDR per serving		11%

Cabbage Rolls (serves 5)

> 1 small cabbage, remove core, remove ten leaves
>   and cook in salted water
> ⅓ cup seitan, chopped into small pieces
> 2 onions. cut mawashigiri (see pg. 141)
> 2 carrots, cut sengiri (see pg. 140)
> kampyo (run water over kampyo to soften it)
> 1 Tbsp oil

In 1 tablespoon of oil, sauté the onion, carrot, and seitan in that order until the color changes. Add 1 teaspoon salt. Place this filling in the cooked cabbage leaves, fold and roll the cabbage leaf, tie with kampyo; this makes ten rolls.

	Protein grams	Methionine/Cystine grams
1 small cabbage (1 lb)	6.4	0.186
⅓ cup seitan	32.1	0.662
2 onions	1.4	0.012
2 carrots	1.2	0.040
Total	41.1	0.900
MDR per serving		3.2%

Boiled Tofu (Yutofu)

> 2 pieces tofu
> 1 chopped scallion
> 3" square kombu
> 1 Tbsp bonita flakes
> lemon juice
> 3-4 Tbsp soy sauce
> orange peel
> 6 cups water

Cut kombu and place in pot with six cups of water and soak thirty minutes. In a porcelain bowl or tea-cup, place 3-4 tablespoons soy sauce (with bits of orange peel) and 1 tablespoon bonita flakes. Place the bowl in the center of the pot. Bring the soup stock to a boil and add the tofu. Bring just to a boil so that tofu is hot, remove the sauce cup, and add scallion to it. (Use soup stock that is left over for another dish. If any sauce is left over, it may be added to make a good cooking dish.)

Bring whole tofu to boil and cut with a bamboo rice paddle or chopstick instead of a metal knife or utensil; it will taste better using the bamboo.

	Protein grams	Methionine/Cystine grams
2 tofu	24.0	0.600
1 scallion	2.4	0.022
1 Tbsp bonita flakes	10.0	0.4 35
3 Tbsp soy sauce	5.7 0.	1.20
Total	42.1	1.177
MDR		107%

Udon Sukiyaki (serves 10)

1½ lbs udon, spaghetti, or home-made noodles

To make "home-made" noodles:
5 cups unbleached white flour
1 tsp salt
1⅓ cups cold water

Mix flour and salt, gradually adding the water. Knead until ear-lobe consistency. Roll out to ⅛" thickness. Flour the top of the dough and fold it over in half. Flour again and fold again—repeating the process until folded dough is about 2-3" in width. This makes it easier to cut the noodles. Be careful not to press too hard on the dough, so that it doesn't stick together. Bring 8 cups water to a boil with 1 teaspoon salt, add noodles. Cook until tender, rinse in cold water, and strain off the water. Pick a handful of noodles and twist them so that they resemble a circle. Place them in a serving bowl.

	Protein grams	Methionine/Cystine grams
5 cups unbleached white flour	108	4.662
MDR per serving		4%

To make the Sukiyaki
5 agé, cut into 3 pieces
10 pieces wheat cutlets, cut in bite-size pieces
3 bunches scallions, cut hasugiri (see pg. 140)
5 medium shiitake mushrooms, soaked 20 minutes, cut in half
10 pieces baked mochi
2 pieces fu, soaked in water, cut in 1" strips
½ head Chinese cabbage, cut in 1" pieces
1 bunch watercress
6" piece kombu
2 heaping Tbsp whole wheat pastry flour
5 cups water
½ Tbsp soy sauce
1 tsp salt

Arrange all the vegetables on a platter. Place the kombu in a pot with 5 cups water and bring to a boil. Add Chinese cabbage, cook for a short time. Add the other ingredients and the noodles. Add the salt and soy sauce, cook for five minutes and serve with béchamel sauce.

To make béchamel sauce: Sauté the pastry flour in one table-spoon oil until it has a nutty fragrance, cool and add the soup stock until it has a creamy consistency. Cook for twenty minutes with 1 teaspoon salt. Add 1 tablespoon wine or sake if desired. Bring the pot with the food to the table. Serve the vegetables on the individual plates and pour the béchamel sauce over them.

To make the wheat cutlet:
1 cup whole wheat pastry flour
5 strips cooked fu (made from either flour)
2 cups tempura batter
2 cups corn meal, bread crumbs, or cracked wheat
tempura oil

Dust strips with pastry flour, then dip into tempura batter, cover with corn meal, and let sit on a plate for about 5 minutes. Deep fry in hot oil (350 degrees) turning over once after strips rise to the top of oil. Cutlets take about 5 minutes to cook. Remove from oil with a strainer or slotted spoon and place in a strainer set inside another pan to catch excess oil before serving.

	Protein grams	Methionine/Cystine grams
5 agé	2.0	0.053
10 wheat cutlets	322.0	13.717
3 bunches scallions	7.2	0.066
5 medium shiitake mushrooms	1.5	0.040
10 baked mochi (2 lbs)	18.0	0.324*
2 fu	64.4	2.743
½ head Chinese cabbage	2.6	0.026*
1 bunch watercress	2.2	0.013*
2 Tbsp whole wheat flour	3.3	0.123
½ Tbsp soy sauce	1.0	0.020
Total	424.21	15.123
MDR per serving		13.7%

* Mochi based on the contents of rice, Chinese cabbage and water-cress based on the figures from *Food Values* by Bowes & Church.

Hijiki Tofu Salad (serves 6)

    1½ blocks tofu, sliced in six pieces
    ⅓ cup dry hijiki
    4 Tbsp white rice miso
    ½ cup white sesame seeds
    1 medium carrot, sengiri (see pg. 140)

Wash sesame seeds, roast in a dry pan, and grind in a suribachi. Wash hijiki four or five times, strain off water, cut in 1" lengths. Heat one tablespoon of oil in a pan, sauté the hijiki well, cover with water, and cook on a high flame until it boils. Lower flame and cook for one hour. Add carrot and continue to cook. When hijiki is tender it is done. Remove the cover and boil off remaining water. Bring 4 cups of water to a boil, add tofu to the water, bring to a boil again and strain. Squeeze any excess water from the tofu, add it to the suribachi with the sesame seeds, and mash the tofu. Also add miso at this time. After the hijiki and carrot have cooled, mix with the tofu mixture. Mix well and serve cold.

	Protein grams	Methionine/Cystine grams
1½ block tofu	12	.30
4 Tbsp rice miso	15	.32
½ cup sesame seeds	38	2.20
1 carrot	1.4	0.06
Total	66.4	2.88
Serving one	11	.48
MDR per serving		7.2%

Soybean Nishime

> 1 cup soybeans, roasted in a dry pan until beans
>   have 2-3 spots of brown color
> 3 medium burdock, cut rangiri (see pg. 139)
> 1 Tbsp sesame oil
> 3 carrots, cut rangiri
> 1 tsp salt
> 1 Tbsp soy sauce
> 2 cups kombu, cut 1" square (soak in water to
>   cover, 10-20 minutes)

Sauté burdock in open pressure cooker until smell is gone, add beans, and sauté for five more minutes. Filter kombu water through a cotton cloth and add to burdock, beans, and kombu. Bring pressure up over a high flame and cook 20 minutes over medium flame. Shut off. After pressure returns to normal, take off cover, add carrot, bring to a boil until pressure is up, then shut off flame and remove from heat. Take off cover, add salt and soy sauce, and cook for 20 more minutes. Toss vegetables and mix bottom and top. Without cover, evaporate the juice. Soybeans are quite yin, so cook them with something yang, like burdock and seaweed, hijiki, onion, carrot, or lotus root. If you have fresh lotus root, add 1½ cups of lotus root to make a very delicious dish.

	Protein grams	Methionine/Cystine grams
1 cup soybeans	79.8	2.382
3 carrots	1.8	0.060
1 Tbsp soy sauce	1.9	0.040
2 cups kombu	14.3	0.500
Total	97.8	2.982
MDR per serving		7.5%

Cutting Styles

Koguchigiri:
Cut into thin rounds.

Koguchigiri Flower:
Cut into thin rounds;
then cut small wedges.

Rangiri:
Cut large diagonal wedges.

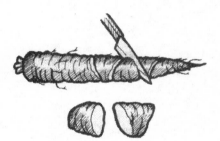

Wagiri:
Cut into rounds;
thicker than in Koguchigiri.

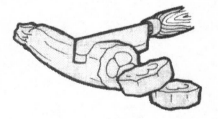

Hasugiri:
Cut diagonal; on the bias.

Sengiri:
Cut each bias section into match-stick size pieces.

Hangetsu:
Cut in half lengthwise.
Then cut Koguchigiri style.

Ichogiri:
Cut in half lengthwise. Cut each half full-length again, then cut Koguchigiri style.

Sainome:
Cut and dice vegetable into pieces about ⅓" thick.

Fan Shape

Tanzaku:
Cut into 1½" long rounds; cut each round on the bias into 4 or 5 pieces; then cut each piece into rectangular slices approximately 1½" x ⅓" x ½".

Sasagaki:
Pencil shave beginning at top of vegetable, rotating vegetable slightly with each cut of knife. May shave thin or thick as desired.

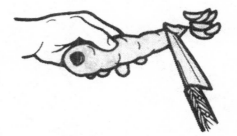

Mawashigiri:
Yin/Yang, moon-shape cut. Cut vegetable in half, lengthwise. Turn on axis and cut into thin moon-shaped slices.

Mejingiri:
Cut in half. Cut thin sections down to about ⅛" from root end across entire vegetable; then slice the opposite direction. Dice into small pieces.

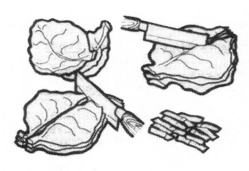

Cabbage strips:
Separate full leaves, stack together, and cut into thin strips.

Quartering and slicing:
Cut into half, then into quarters, and slice thick or thin as desired.

Bibliography

Aihara, Cornellia, *Chico-San Cookbook*, by Chico-San Inc., Chico, CA, 1972

Aihara, Cornellia, *Do of Cooking*, by G.O.M.F., Chico, CA, 1973

Aihara, Herman, *Macrobiotics: An Invitation to Health and Happiness*, by G.O.M.F., Oroville, CA, 1971

Altman, Nathaniel, *Eating for Life, a Book about Vegetarianism*, by The Theosophical Pub. House, Wheaton, Ill., 1973

Kirschman, John D., *Nutrition Almanac*, by Nutrition Search, Minneapolis, Minn., 1973

McCarrison, Sir Robert & Sinclair, H.M., *Nutrition and Health*, by Faber & Faber Ltd., London, 1936

Miller, D. Carey, *Nutritive Values of Hawaii Foods*, by Hawaii Agriculture Experiment Station, University of Hawaii, 1960

Null, Gary and Steve, *Protein for Vegetarians*, by Pyramid Communications Inc., N.Y., 1974

Ohsawa, George, *Philosophy of Oriental Medicine*, by G.O.M.F., Chico, CA, 1991

Ohsawa, George, *Unique Principle,* by G.O.M.F., 1972

U.S. Government, Dept. of Agriculture, *Year Book of Agriculture, 1959*, Amino Acid Content of Foods Home, Economic Research Report No. 4, 1957, Composition of Foods Used in Far Eastern Countries, Agriculture Handbook No. 34, 1952

Useful Information

Measurements

1 teaspoon = ⅓ tablespoon	16 tablespoons = 1 cup
1 Tablespoon = 3 teaspoons	1 cup = 8 ounces
2 Tablespoons = 1 ounce	1 cup = ½ pint
2 Tablespoons = ⅛ cup	2 cups = 1 pint
4 Tablespoons = ¼ cup	2 pints = 1 quart
5 ⅓ Tablespoons = ⅓ cup	8 pints = 1 gallon
8 Tablespoons = ½ cup	4 quarts = 1 gallon

Gram Conversion Tables for Different Foods

Item:	Water, Sake Rice vinegar	Soy sauce Miso	Salt	Kuzu Arrowroot	Wheat Flour	Oil
1 tsp	5	6	4	3	3	4
1 Tbsp	15	18	12	10	8	13
1 cup	200	230	160	120	100	180

1 ounce = approx. 28 grams of liquid or dry measure

1 pound = approx. 454 grams of liquid or dry measure

Recipe Abbreviations

lbs = pounds	oz = ounces
tsp = teaspoons	" = inches
Tbsp = Tablespoons	w.w. = whole wheat

Suggested Amounts to Serve 5 People

½ chicken or ½ lb chicken
1 whole fish (head and tail included) = 1½ lbs
Slices of fish: a little more than ½ lb
Shrimp and other shellfish: ½ lb
Eggs: 4 eggs
Tofu: 2 blocks
Vegetables: 1-2 lbs

Kuzu Sauce Measurements for 5 People

1-2 cups soup stock or water
1 Tbsp sake
1 tsp salt
1 Tbsp soy sauce
1 tsp to 1 Tbsp kuzu or arrowroot
1 Tbsp to 3 Tbsp water

Clear Soup Measurements for 5-6 People

3 cups soup stock
3 cups plain water
1 Tbsp sake
2 tsp salt
1 tsp soy sauce

Sweet-Sour Kuzu Sauce for 5 People

1 cup water
1-2 Tbsp yinnie (malt) syrup*
½ tsp salt
2 Tbsp soy sauce
3 Tbsp Chico-San rice vinegar
1 Tbsp sake
1 Tbsp arrowroot or kuzu

*Note: Raisin syrup, amasake, juices, or juice concentrates may be substituted for yinnie syrup in recipes.

Index

Other Books from the
George Ohsawa Macrobiotic Foundation

Acid Alkaline Companion - Carl Ferré; 2009; 121 pp.

Acid and Alkaline - Herman Aihara; 1986; 121 pp.

As Easy As 1, 2, 3 - Pamela Henkel and Lee Koch; 1990; 176 pp.

Basic Macrobiotic Cooking, 20th Anniversary Edition - Julia Ferré; 2007; 275 pp.

Book of Judo - George Ohsawa; 1990; 150 pp.

Cancer and the Philosophy of the Far East - George Ohsawa; 1981; 165 pp.

Essential Guide to Macrobiotics - Carl Ferré; 2011; 131 pp.

Essential Ohsawa - George Ohsawa, edited by Carl Ferré; 1994; 238 pp.

Food and Intuition 101 Volume 1: Awakening Intuition - Julia Ferré; 2012; 226 pp.

Food and Intuition 101 Volume 2: Developing Intuition - Julia Ferré; 2013; 242 pp.

French Meadows Cookbook - Julia Ferré; 2008; 275 pp.

Macrobiotics: An Invitation to Health and Happiness - George Ohsawa; 1971; 128 pp.

Philosophy of Oriental Medicine - George Ohsawa; 1991; 153 pp.

Practical Guide to Far Eastern Macrobiotic Medicine - George Ohsawa; 2010; 279 pp.

Zen Cookery - G.O.M.F.; 1985; 140 pp.

Zen Macrobiotics, Unabridged Edition - George Ohsawa, edited by Carl Ferré; 1995; 206 pp.

A wide selection of macrobiotic books is available from the George Ohsawa Macrobiotic Foundation, P.O. Box 3998, Chico, CA 95965; 530-566-9765. Order toll free: 800-232-2372. Or, you may visit *www.OhsawaMacrobiotics.com* for all books and PDF downloads of many books.

Made in the USA
Columbia, SC
28 November 2017